playing slow pitch softball

Robert G. Hoehn

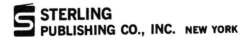 STERLING
PUBLISHING CO., INC. NEW YORK

STERLING SPORTS BOOKS

Advanced Tennis
Baseball
Basketball
Fine Points of Tennis
Getting Started in Tennis
Girls' Basketball
Girls' Gymnastics
Golf Explained

Handball Basics
Junior Tennis
Playing with a Football
Racquetball
Soccer the Way the Pros Play
Start Golf Young
Warm Up for Little League Baseball
Warm Up for Soccer

DEDICATION

To Ethel Hoehn Edsall. This one's for you.

Contents

Play ball!

Introduction

Riddle: What do a batter who swings under the ball and slow pitch softball leagues have in common? Answer: Both are popping up everywhere throughout the U.S.

In Sacramento, California, alone, slow pitch has grown to more than 600 teams in the last three years. While top fast pitch teams drop from competition, slow pitch teams grow in popularity. Men's and women's slow pitch tournaments are drawing large numbers of people to the parks, and senior slow pitch leagues for those fifty years of age or older have helped skyrocket interest. Slow pitch softball holds no magical spell over its participants, but it does provide the felicities of relaxation, fun and satisfaction.

This book will prepare you, the player, for action. It has two major purposes:

● To help the player improve and find success.

● To serve as a guide for both the beginning and veteran player.

What, then, can you expect to find in this book?

First, you'll see why slow pitch has increased in popularity, why players wait anxiously for the season to begin, and the differences between fast pitch and slow pitch (style of play, rules, etc.).

Second, you'll learn how to prepare for the upcoming season. You'll discover ways to get your throwing arm and legs into shape, how to find your position, and how to use practice time wisely. The chapter titled "Slow Pitch Drills and Games for Everyone" includes drills for 2, 3, 4 or 5 players.

Third, you'll receive batting tips and drills which will help you become a better hitter.

Fourth, you'll get practical suggestions and drills for making accurate throws and perfecting your fielding technique.

Fifth, you'll see how to pitch, how to play different infield positions, how to play the outfield, and how to become a good base runner.

Sixth, you'll receive tips on how to score runs and how to build a strong defense.

The final chapter lists recommended guidelines for playing slow pitch which will aid not only players, but managers and sponsors as well.

Make Way for Slow Pitch

Welcome to one of the fastest growing sports around. As a player you'll treat yourself to plenty of running, throwing, fielding, and hitting. As a fan you'll see action-packed softball at its very, very best.

What's So Special about Slow Pitch?

Ask Uncle Walter. See Cousin Louise. Or talk to Mr. Finch down the street. They'll all tell you the same thing. Slow pitch stands out because nearly everyone hits the ball somewhere, and nothing thrills a player more than making solid contact with a pitched ball. It's just plain fun coming to bat three or four times in a regular seven-inning game. You can relax and swing easy. Best of all, you don't have to worry about hard sliders and fast-breaking curves—they don't exist in slow pitch. The biggest challenge a hitter faces is when to pull the trigger; that is, at what point to swing the bat.

Why Players Are Turning to Slow Pitch

Did you ever see the bumper sticker that reads "If it feels good, do it"? Well, that statement just about sums up how most people feel about playing slow pitch. But having fun isn't the only drawing card. Here are five more reasons why slow pitch is growing in popularity:

● Exercise. Running about. Fielding, throwing, and hitting. Slow pitch lets you do all of these things. You can go easy or you can work your tail off. How hard you work depends entirely on your reason for playing.

● Getting together with friends and enjoying each other's company. Conversations range from painting the house to catching lunker bass. Even a shy player occasionally gets excited and shouts "Mine! Mine!" or "Take it! Take it!"

No one talks suicide. No one worries about killer bees carrying the light poles away. Players seem happy just to mingle together, exchange thoughts, and laugh when a misjudged ball lands 20 feet behind a player.

● Slow pitch isn't a private institution. People of all ages take part. Any healthy male or female can play. In many areas around the country, a person fifty years of age or older can join a senior slow pitch team.

Women do all right, too. They can play on all-girl teams or join a coed league which requires each team to keep an equal number of boys and girls on the field at the same time. That's not all. Some recreational programs include the entire family in low-level competition slow pitch. Clearly then, the only thing keeping a person from playing slow pitch, short of poor health, is not wanting to play.

● It takes much less time to play than fast pitch. Many leagues set a time limit, say one hour or seven innings, whichever comes first.

● There's action galore. Things happen fast. Thrilling plays follow one another like ducks swimming across a pond. You might see a hot liner rip off a fielder's glove or a runner lose a shoe rounding second base. Indeed, slow pitch provides enough entertainment, exercise—and suspense —to keep you satisfied for a long time.

What's a Big Difference Between Fast Pitch and Slow Pitch?

In a word, hitting.

Some fast pitch players who try to hit slow pitch for the first time find the going tough—and embarrassing. A slow, Alley-Oop delivery can upset the timing of a fast pitch player. Here's what can happen. A strong, free-swinging batter steps up to home plate. The pitcher winds and delivers. The ball doesn't zoom across home plate. Instead it climbs and climbs and climbs. Then gravity takes over and sends the ball spinning down toward home plate. The batter's eyes grow large as saucers. Arm muscles tighten under the strain of whipping the bat around.

A swing and miss. A big strike. And a big red face.

It happens. It happens often. The player either returns to fast pitch or sticks around to learn the recipe for hitting slow pitch, which is simply 1 part skill, 3 parts timing, and 6 parts patience.

Go by the Rules

Another difference between slow pitch and fast pitch is the rules. Rules call for a change in playing style.

Let's look at eight major rule differences between slow pitch and fast pitch. They are as follows:

1. A fast pitch team fields nine players per team. A slow pitch team fields ten players. The tenth player, the second short fielder, is known as the rover.

2. You can bunt in fast pitch, not so in slow pitch.

3. Both leading off base and stealing are okay in fast pitch. A player can do neither in slow pitch.

4. The batter can swing down or chop at the ball in fast pitch. The chop swing is not allowed in slow pitch.

5. The strike zone is over home plate between the top of a batter's knees and the line of his armpits in fast pitch. In slow pitch, the strike zone is over home plate between a batter's knees and shoulders.

6. In slow pitch, every pitch must attain a height of between 3 and 10 feet above the point of release before reaching the plate.

7. The pitcher must have both feet in contact with the pitcher's rubber before beginning his windup in fast pitch. In slow pitch the pitcher may touch the rubber with only one foot before beginning his windup.

8. An illegal pitch results in a ball for the batter and a base for the runner in fast pitch. In slow pitch, an illegal pitch results in a ball for the batter, but the runners do not advance.

Know the rules and be aware of new changes. Don't hold up the game for a rule interpretation. This wastes time, creates confusion, and prolongs the game.

For a complete set of slow pitch rules, write to:

Amateur Softball Association of America
P.O. Box 11437
Oklahoma City, Oklahoma 73111

Is Slow Pitch for You?

"You can stand on your head, whistle 'Dixie,' and hit slow pitch at the same time." That's what some people think. Absurd. Not everyone knows "Dixie" or can whistle. But the message rings clear—you don't have to be a superstar to play slow pitch. If you can swing a bat, wave your glove at a fly ball, and limp around the bases, then you can play slow pitch.

After a game or two, take the following quiz. Check which of the items you feel are true.

● The pitcher tried to deck you with a high, inside fast ball.

● The pitcher is rubbing a foreign substance on the ball, like salad oil, hair tonic, or tobacco juice.

● Slow pitch is too slow.

● The second short fielder is too tall.

● The umpire calls too many high pitches strikes.

If you checked any of the items, forget about playing slow pitch. Try checkers or marbles or pinochle.

But, hopefully, this advice is for someone else, not you.

Putting It All Together

If you like to stay active and have fun, then slow pitch is for you. It's one of the few team sports which allow both boys and girls to participate on an equal basis. Young or old, male or female, novice or experienced, everyone is welcome.

So come out and toss the ball around. Join one of the most popular games in town.

How to Succeed
in Slow Pitch
(by Really Trying)

Just How Good Are You?

A tough question, isn't it?

If you answer "I'm great" it sounds like you're bragging. A reply of "Gee, I don't know," falls short and says nothing about your ability. How, then, will you ever find out? Well, the next time you take the field, look behind you. If you notice a TV cameraman following you around, you're great.

Let's face it. This probably won't happen. There aren't that many super players who consistently throw bullets, hit rockets, or run like a cheetah. Most players are average to good which means they can throw, hit, and run well enough to play slow pitch for many moons.

An average slow pitch player is interested in having fun, not impressing anyone. So when somebody asks "How good are you?" ignore the question. No matter what you say the person won't believe you anyway.

Goals, Goals, and More Goals

Just think. You can play slow pitch for many, many years. There's really no magic formula. As long as you stay healthy and happy, you can't miss. You already know the recipe for good health, which is daily exercise, proper diet, and plenty of rest. And you're aware that a well-tuned body seldom breaks down.

Happiness is easy to gauge, too. Anything from a grand-slam home run to a pretty sunset can bring a smile to a player's face. Conversely, a wild throw which allows the winning run to score can turn that smile upside down. How can you keep smiling most of the time? Simply by doing what you set out to do, that is, decide before the season begins what goals you want to reach.

A wise player sets realistic goals. For example, an outfielder with a weak arm doesn't plan to throw out very many base runners. If the same outfielder hits the ball hard, going for 10 homers a season may be within reach.

When the slow pitch season draws near, find an empty notebook, sharpen a few pencils, sit down, and start to list the goals you plan to reach. In another section of your notebook keep a record of each game, including date, time, and location of game. Record times at bat (AB), hits, runs scored, sacrifice flies (SF), runs batted in (RBI), and strikeouts (K). Write down anything you wish to remember. List everything you do, both at bat and on the field.

At the end of the season, place the final averages and totals on a season goal chart (see page 140). Don't limit yourself to batting goals. Remember, you spend half of the game patrolling on defense. A defensive goal might be to play five straight games without booting the ball or to keep all throws shoulder high, to the glove side. Let these points guide you in the right direction:

● Keep each goal within your grasp. Don't expect to hit thirty home runs in ten games unless you've done it a few times before. Sure, there are slow pitch players who hit over 200 home runs a season. But these guys play over 100 games a year, including several tournaments throughout the United States. They're famous for sending the ball into orbit.

● Make your goals challenging. Let them give your playing ability a true test, but don't go wild and think you can lick the world. If you're not strong enough to hit the ball a country mile, forget the home runs. Go for singles.

● Keep silent. Don't tell everybody in town you're going to bat .500 this year. Let it be a surprise. Besides, there's always one person who will laugh in your face if you wind up hitting only .499!

Don't Outrun Your Pacemaker

Look over the following list of words. Pick out the word which holds the most danger for a slow pitch player.

1. glove

2. bat

3. ball

4. urge

Did you select Number 4, "urge"? Good. That's the one.

The word urge is a real dandy. When you begin playing slow pitch, something takes over your body. It's strange, almost like a warm rush of new energy crying to get out. This is urge. Your leg and arm muscles come alive. You feel as though you can reach out and punch a hole in the moon with your finger.

Urge has a way of telling your body to go, go, go. But be on guard. Give in to urge and you risk arm strain on that long, hard throw you're dying to make. Set urge free and you chance pulling a leg muscle trying to stretch a single into a double.

After a long layoff, muscles need time to stretch back into action. A quick turn in the wrong direction or a long, hard throw is a surefire way to injure or pull a muscle. The human body, like a speed trap, can lead you astray. For example, let's say you haven't picked up a ball since last season. After five minutes of playing catch, your arm feels strong enough to fire a ball through a brick wall. Your arm cries out "Throw faster. Throw faster." You do. Tomorrow comes. And with it an arm sore enough to be pronounced dead. Overexposure hurts. So do yourself a favor: go easy.

Replace urge with good sense. Think before you act. Take it easy and warm up gradually. Let your energy carry you along at a slow, easy pace.

Winning Isn't Everything

Slow pitch and high-scoring games go hand in hand. It's not unusual for a team to score twenty or thirty or more runs in a single game.

For instance, take a Class C women's slow pitch team from Lansing, Michigan. They lost a game 53 to 0. That's an average of seven and one half runs per inning. Fortunately, the game didn't go seven innings. The game lasted only two innings before being called because of a "mercy" rule.

Think about it. That's an average of twenty-six and one half runs per inning. Mercy came too late. The score stood 37 to 0 after the first inning.

There's a great lesson to learn here. Simply, if you think winning is everything, don't play slow pitch in Lansing, Michigan. Or anywhere else.

Keep this in mind whenever you take the field. That way you'll be less likely to hurt yourself and more likely to have fun.

What's Wrong with Being Nice?

Leo Durocher in his book *Nice Guys Finish Last* says that if you surround yourself with ball players considered really nice guys, you're going to finish down in the cellar with them. He, of course, was talking about major league baseball players. He further states that if you're in professional sports and you don't care whether you win or lose, you are going to finish last.

Well, in slow pitch you can field ten of the nicest people in town—and still win! But this is amateur sports, not professional. And that's one of the great things about slow pitch: You can kid around, have a laugh or two, and still score a ton of runs.

Oh, sure, occasionally some guy with a loud voice, a flashy glove, and miles of experience announces that he's going to tear up the league. More often than not the only thing he tears is his pants while sliding into second base. There's no place in slow pitch for the "I come to kill" player. But this doesn't mean you shouldn't try hard to win. You owe it to yourself, teammates, and sponsor to do the best you can. But remember—if it stops being fun, do something else.

Butterflies Appear in the Spring

Hitting a high, lofting pitch is not only challenging, but fun. However, most players say they're a trifle nervous the first time they come to bat.

Butterflies invade the stomach of every ball player at one time or another. Even players with 20 or 30 years of experience admit butterflies appear prior to game time and may hang around for an inning or two. There's no cure for butterflies, no anti-fluttering pills to stop their wings from pounding. When you catch them, they're yours for as long as you choose to swing a bat, catch a ball, or jog around the bases.

They do, however, serve a purpose. The next time you strike out or fumble the ball, don't take all of the credit. Pass some along to your butterflies. After all, people sympathize with players who are kind to animals, especially butterflies.

In short, don't worry about being worried.

Getting Insight Information

Slow pitch is a simple game. It involves only hitting, fielding, throwing, and running, right? Wrong. There's more, much more. For instance, consider the word "insight." Psychologists tell us that insight occurs when a person suddenly sees the answer to a problem. They call this an "Aha! I have it!" experience.

Suppose someone gives you a puzzle to solve. You try and try, but can't find a solution. Then lightning strikes. The answer smacks you between the eyes like a rake handle. This is insight. Did the answer come out of a clear blue sky? It seems so, but chances are that prior experience in a similar situation helped you find the solution.

All right, you know what insight means. Now let's see how it applies to slow pitch. In Roseville, California, the slow pitch league uses a rubber disk 3 feet in diameter to cover home plate. A pitched ball that hits any part of the disk is a strike.

A clever pitcher thinks "Aha! I'll toss the ball just far enough to nip the front edge of the disk. The batter will most likely swing and miss or hit the ball weakly onto the ground." Notice how the pitcher combines insight and strategy to solve the problem of getting the batter out.

An alert batter thinks "Aha! I'll move to the front of home plate or run up and swing before the ball drops." Again, see how insight and strategy work together to help the batter make solid contact with the ball.

Keep your eyes open and watch for holes in your opponent's web. Let insight (and strategy) put you a step ahead of the other guy.

A Laugh an Inning

What's better than watching summer reruns on television? That's easy. Either join a slow pitch team or sit in the stands and take in the sights. Funny things happen on the field. Here are 4 beauties of gem quality:

GEM NUMBER 1

Batter hits a fly ball into center field. Center fielder watches ball carefully, paying special attention to wind speed and direction. Fielder circles under ball and reaches up to make catch. Plop! Ball lands 20 feet behind fielder. (Manager shakes head, turns around, kicks the dirt.)

GEM NUMBER 2

Runner at third, 1 out. Batter hits fly ball to left field. When fielder catches ball, runner tags, and sprints home. Fielder cuts loose with a tremendous throw. Ball sails over backstop and into the night. (Manager shakes head, turns around, mumbles something.)

GEM NUMBER 3

Tether-ball pole in right field, foul territory. Batter hits fly ball near pole. Right fielder (right-handed) races over, reaches out for catch, misses ball, grabs pole with right arm, and spins around twice before falling to ground. (Manager shakes head, turns around, smiles.)

GEM NUMBER 4

Outfielder misjudges fly ball. Ball bounces off player's head. Player stumbles, falls down, and loses cap. A fan calls out, "That's using your head!" (Manager laughs out loud.)

Infielders help share in the buffoonery. It's worth a laugh seeing a pitcher juggle a hard smash hit back through the box, bouncing from hand to hand like a hot penny.

Double-play situations tickle the funny bone, too. For example, a runner on first, none out. The pitcher looks over the infield, smiles, taps his glove three times, and shouts out "Let's get two! Let's get two!" The batter hits a two-hopper to the right of the shortstop. The shortstop makes a super backhand play, straightens up, and throws the ball a mile over the second baseman's head.

Fans manage to get in a few good shots, too. These popular outbursts spring from the stands:

- *Batter swings and misses:* "Hey, batter. Watch out! The pitcher has a great change up."

- *Batter swings and misses:* "You're swinging up on the ball, batter."

- *Pitcher makes sky-high delivery:* "C'mon, pitch, bring the ball up where the batter can see it."

- *Infielder after making an error:* "Don't worry, fielder. Anyone can make an error and look like a silly jerk."

And so on.

Player or fan, if you don't laugh, you're not enjoying life. You just can't lose watching a slow pitch game. And you can bet it beats anything you'll see on television.

From Ouija Board to Home Plate

There's magic in a beautiful sunset. That's what nature writers say. There's magic in underwater sea life. Ask any scuba diver. With so much magic going around, you'd think some of it would rub off on slow pitch players, wouldn't you? Well, it does. At least that's what some players choose to believe. For them, superstition, a kind of magic, plays a big part.

Did you know there are players who refuse to wash their socks? They wear the same pair throughout the season. Why? A clean sock, they think, might change their luck from good to bad.

Strange beliefs and superstitions go together. A player might not reveal a superstition fearing it will snap the magical spell. Maybe a player believes that chewing only one kind of gum, say spearmint, will guarantee a fat batting average. If somebody else finds out, the magic might lose its sweetness like the gum that the player's chewing. Players hang on to their beliefs. They aren't about to let their secrets slip away.

Maybe you don't believe in magical power or a mystical force strong enough to raise your batting average. Or maybe you'd like to try a superstition, but don't know where to look. You're in luck. Now you can select a superstition from the following list and try it for the entire season. If it fails to bring positive results, choose another. Keep picking until yo find one that works.

SELECT-O-SUPERSTITION

● Put on your game shoes, left foot first.

● Never step on a gum wrapper or ice-cream stick while running from first to second.

● Never let your team's pitcher stand between you and the bat rack.

● Say hello to the opposing catcher *before* stepping into the batter's box.

● Keep a broken pencil in the left rear pocket of your pants.

● Hold one half of a toothpick on the right side of your tongue while batting.

● Chant "Hum, babe" two times before catching a fly ball.

● After the pitcher releases the ball, close your eyes, count to five, and open them before the batter swings.

● When you take a drink, never swallow the first gulp. Spit it over your left shoe.

● When you see a friend, wave with your bare hand. Never show your glove hand.

Good sense, conscience, and fear of the unknown combine forces to hold this list to ten superstitions. But don't let that stop you. If you can't find one you like, make up one of your own.

What Are the Odds?

Webster's New International Dictionary defines "odd" as "unusual" or "strange." We also use it to mean uneven, queer, erratic, funny, crazy, cracked, and so on.

Slow pitch players often do odd things. These quirks or peculiarities are also known as idiosyncrasies. Does this mean that the players are crazy? Not really. Players sometimes act peculiarly because it helps them relax, relieve tension, and chase those butterflies away. Some pound rocks into the ground with the fat end of the bat; others suck in their stomachs, tighten facial muscles, and crane their necks. None of these actions appear weird on the playing field. However, they might draw a stare or two in Macy's lingerie department.

Simple gestures go unnoticed. Nobody thinks twice about a player pulling a cap bill down several times before stepping into the batter's box. When it's your turn to bat, feel free to tug at your ear or pick lint out of your pocket. Do anything you like. If it makes you play better, you can't go wrong.

Let's See if You're a Success

How successful will you be in slow pitch? It depends on three things—desire, dedication, and how well you read this chapter.

You're now going to take a test covering the material in this chapter. Relax. Don't be nervous. Your score will tell you whether or not to spend money on a glove, bat, and shoes.

Pick up a pencil and number 1 through 10 on a piece of paper. Make a plus (+) for true and circle (o) for false. Don't look for the answers listed after the quiz. And don't sneak a peek back in the chapter (unless you're bent on making a perfect score).

SUCCESS TEST

1. If you consistently throw bullets or hit rockets, you'd be better off in the army.

2. Nothing runs as fast as a cheetah, except a cheetah.

3. The best way to cure stomach butterflies is to drink two glasses of water while singing "Take Me Out to the Ball Game."

4. The most dangerous word to a slow pitch player is egru.

5. If you haven't hit a home run in the last five years, make it your personal goal to lead the league in home runs this year.

6. RBI means "Rotten Batter Indeed!"

7. The best way to suddenly see the answer to a problem is by looking at someone else's paper.

8. A player with a "Kill! Kill!" attitude should bat fourth in the lineup.

9. A smart sporting goods dealer will carry a large supply of rabbits' feet, four-leaf clovers, and horseshoes.

10. A player who grimaces and slaps both legs at the same time is probably choking on a wad of gum.

ANSWERS TO SUCCESS TEST

1. + (Or in the National Guard)

2. + (According to a cheetah)

3. o (Lie down, close your eyes, and go to sleep)

4. o (True, if you read from right to left)

5. o (People would only think you're a show-off)

6. o (Means Really Big Inning. Or is it Runs Batted In?)

7. o (There are other ways, like writing answers on the palm of your hand or on your shirt sleeve)

8. o (Should bat first, second, third, fourth, fifth . . . . . .)

9. o (No, a smart dealer will order a huge supply of lucky shorts and number 7 jerseys)

10. o (May be coughing up a butterfly)

SCORING IS AS FOLLOWS:

10—9 correct ... A true success story
8—7 correct ... A success story
6—5 correct ... A story
4—0 correct ... Grab your glove and play ball. This test doesn't prove anything.

Putting It All Together

Play slow pitch. Forget about how good you think you are, or for that matter, how good others think you are. You're in it for fun and pleasure, not fame and fortune.

Pace yourself and you'll last forever. Set reasonable goals to reach one at a time. Then go for bigger stakes.

Try hard, keep smiling, and sprinkle salt over your left shoulder if you like. Do whatever you think will bring you success.

Preparing for the Coming Season

The quiz in the first chapter and test in the second chapter gave you the green light to play slow pitch. Now you're ready. Nothing can stand in your way. So, there's only one thing left to do—gather what you need for the upcoming season.

Get Your Equipment Together

Okay, you need equipment. But what kind should you get for playing slow pitch? Here's a pre-season checklist to help you out:

● Get a glove big enough to haul in fly balls and stop fast-moving ground balls. Some big leaguers go for jumbo-sized gloves or mitts, especially nervous catchers trying to flag down knuckle balls. You can relax. This isn't the big leagues. A goliath-sized glove is heavy, awkward, and hard to slam down when you make an error.

Find an inexpensive glove, but one that looks and feels good. Take your time, there's no rush. And if you're lucky, you'll run across a special sale on softball equipment. Slow down when you come to a garage sale. People sell everything from crutches to cricket cages. Play your cards right and you might steal a classy old glove for a couple of bucks (or best offer).

● The chapter, *Stepping Up to the Plate*, tells you how to select a bat. But pay heed to one thing—if another player breaks your bat, don't swear, yell, or cry out in pain. Use your head. Make sure the next bat you select is aluminum.

● Buy a nice-fitting, well-made pair of baseball shoes. Comfort is the key. A word of caution, though. Don't wear a cheap pair of shoes. They won't last and blisters pop up like corks from wine bottles.

Don't buy the first pair you see. Check around and compare prices. Then come up with a pair you'll be proud to shine. Also, remember to wear socks. They'll protect your feet, keep them warm, and hold down the blister population.

● A clown looks funny wearing a hat that covers half of his face. So does a slow pitch player. Unless you play for the Courtland Comics or the Billingham Bumpkins, you'd be better off wearing a cap that fits.

Most sports shops carry an attractive, lightweight baseball cap with an adjustable plastic strip across the back. Many players prefer this style over the heavier cloth caps. Don't set your mind on blue if your sponsor prefers yellow. The sponsor has the last word. After all, he's the one who forks over the money for caps and jerseys.

● Should you wear long pants or short pants? Should you wear sliding pads, knee pads, or both? Should you wear a short-sleeve jersey or long-sleeve jersey? Should you wear white socks or colored socks? Let's tackle these questions one at a time.

First, if you fall down often or like to slide, wear long pants.

Second, if you slide on your knees or stumble around the bases like an elephant, wear both knee and sliding pads.

Third, if a long-sleeve jersey restricts your throwing ability because it doesn't let your biceps "breathe," put on a short-sleeve jersey.

Fourth, wear any color socks you want. If you're wearing long-legged pants, it won't make a hill of beans. Nobody will see them anyway.

Now that you're properly attired, let's talk about your body.

Getting Your Body to Cooperate

Playing slow pitch wakes up your body processes. You feel super from head to toe. New blood seems to rush through your veins. Your legs beg to run the bases. Your throwing arm cries to play catch. Everything is beautiful. You want to jump out of bed in the morning and jog 5 miles before breakfast. Sounds good, doesn't it? Admittedly, a bit farfetched, but still a nice way to start the day.

Will your body really feel like a potpourri of bliss? Yes, especially if you treat it with respect and kindness. But here's the problem —some players force their bodies into action before warming up properly. Awful things happen. Tendons snap. Muscles pop. Bones crack. This breakfast-cereal melody is not the kind of music players wish to hear.

The next two sections will show you how to put your arms and legs in a playing mood.

Prepare Your Legs for Running

Slow pitch might not be the roughest sport in town, but injuries do occur. A slight turn in the wrong direction or fast start from home plate can keep a player out of action for a long time. Nobody wants to watch a game from the bench while nursing a sprained knee or strained back. Yet injuries are part of the game and will be around for as long as players overuse and abuse their muscles.

Before you charge onto the field, consider two things: (1) What you'll be doing—throwing, running, etc. (2) How far you should go; that is, know your limitations.

Let's begin by getting your legs ready for competition. Here are three excellent (5 to 10 minute) exercises which will stretch out leg muscles and make them more flexible.

Illus. 1a and 1b. The reach: plant one leg on ground with knee straight, step ahead on other foot and bend forward with hands on knee.

EXERCISE 1: REACH (Illus. 1a and b)

1. Plant your right foot on the ground, keeping knee straight.

2. Step ahead with your left foot as far as possible.

3. Rest both hands on your left knee and bend forward.

4. Hold this position for five seconds. Repeat five times with each leg.
   This exercise stretches the calf-muscle, or the fleshy back part of the leg below the knee.

Illus. 2a.   **Illus. 2b.**

EXERCISE 2: STRETCH (Illus. 2a and b)

1. Plant your left foot, keeping the leg straight.

2. Set your right heel on a bench. Hold your leg straight and point your toe.

3. Bend forward *slowly*. Try to touch your instep or toes with both hands.

4. Hold the position for five seconds. Repeat five times with each leg.
   This exercise stretches the hamstring muscle and the tendons located in back of the knee.

Illus. 3.   The lean back.

EXERCISE 3: LEAN BACK (Illus. 3)

1. Kneel down. Hold your hands to the side.

2. Lean back slowly. Go back as far as you can. Try to see the ground behind you.

3. Hold this position for five seconds. Repeat eight to ten times.

This exercise stretches the quadriceps muscles (front of the thigh). They start near the hip and end below the knee.

There are other ways to stretch out leg muscles. Talk to other players and find out the kind of stretching exercises they do before practice or a game. But make the exercises fit you—don't be a copycat. Some players may need twenty or thirty minutes to warm up but you may need only ten. You be the judge.

Most players say a warm, springy feeling tells them when muscles are warmed up and ready to go. A safety slogan might be, "Don't do a thing until you feel the spring."

Getting the Throwing Arm Ready

Nothing hurts like a sore arm. It takes the romance out of playing. A painful, throbbing arm wants only one thing—to be left alone to die. Who gets a sore arm? Any player who neglects to stretch out his arm muscles or warm up properly before making long, hard throws.

Push-ups, pull-ups, and bar hangs do a nice job of stretching these muscles. Unless you're from Mars or Pluto, doing a push-up or pull-up is nothing new. But, here again, common sense should be your guide. Don't tire yourself going for a world record. Do just enough to arouse that warm, springy feeling that signals you into action.

Illus. 4. Let's see how a bar hang will help you.

EXERCISE 4: BAR HANG (Illus. 4)

1. Hang from an overhead bar with both hands. Don't touch the ground with your feet.

2. Let your arms support your body weight.

3. Release the non-throwing hand from the bar.

4. Hold yourself there for 5 seconds. Repeat three or four times.

If you can't find an overhead bar, grab a backstop or sideline fence, tuck your legs, and hold on. Check the fence carefully for any rough edges or metal slivers. Protect your hands and fingers as well as your arm.

Warm up slowly. Throw easy. Don't make a long, hard throw until you've warmed up properly. You'll run across warning signs like these often in this book. Study them. Remember them. Follow them. And if you respect your arm and treat it like an old friend, it will seldom let you down.

What Position Should You Play?

Are you a terrific first baseman? Can you play third base like a pro? Or do you think the pitcher's mound would make a nice home?

Perhaps you really don't know where to play. Or maybe it doesn't make any difference as long as you see action. Don't worry, there's a way to find out where you belong. Look at the following chart. It lists seven items that go into the makeup of a slow pitch player.

Make a chart like this for yourself on a pad or sheet of paper.

RATING CHART

Item	5 Excellent	4 Good	3 Average	2 Poor
Speed Afoot				
Reflexes				
Body Strength				
Height				
Throwing Speed				
Throwing Accuracy				
Fielding Ability				

Rate the way you feel about yourself. Place a check mark for each item under the heading which you think describes you best (Excellent to Poor). Notice the point values: Excellent 5; Good 4; Average 3; and

Poor 2. Now add the check marks in the Excellent column and multiply by 5. For example, if you counted 3 marks, the Excellent column would total 15 points.

Do the same for the other columns. Multiply check marks by the given point values and write down the final total. Don't lose it; you'll need it in a few moments.

Suppose a tiny voice inside your head whispers, "Play third. You're a natural." Will you drop everything, sprint over to third base, and set up camp? Hopefully, no. Tiny voices sometimes lie. You need to know what type of player is best suited for each position. The following rundown may be a big help to you:

CATCHER

Big, strong and aggressive. A team leader. Determined to block home plate and stop runs from scoring. (20 points minimum)

PITCHER

A real hustler, not afraid to back up bases. Good control, throws mostly strikes. Alert, quick reflexes, an excellent fielder. (25 points minimum)

FIRST BASE

Fast footwork, fine arm, excellent fielder. Able to catch high and low throws. Fast reflexes, very quick hands. Should be fairly tall. (25 points minimum)

SECOND BASE

Excellent fielder, quick hands, and fast reflexes. One of the best fielders on the team. (28 points minimum)

SHORTSTOP

Strong, accurate arm. Fast, quick hands and speedy reflexes. Gets rid of ball quickly, able to throw from any position. Top fielder. (34 points minimum)

THIRD BASE

Tough, good fielder, strong arm, and quick hands. (26 points minimum)

OUTFIELDER (including rover)

Good speed. Strong, accurate arm with outstanding ability to catch fly balls and line drives. (26 points minimum)

Compare your rating chart point totals with the minimum points listed for each position. Do you notice something interesting? Look again. Now do you see it? That's right. According to the rating chart, you can play more than one position. See? You're worth a bunch more than you thought.

You don't need charts and rundowns to show you where to play. No, once you take the field, a natural force will point you in the right direction. And, in many cases, your team manager will be on the opposite end of the pointer.

A Word about Practice

No two players feel exactly the same way about practice. One may choose to work out two or three times a week with only a couple of friends. Another might prefer to practice during team workouts. The expression "practice makes perfect" says it all. If you want to improve, practice. There is no other way. Nobody ever became a great pitcher by tossing paper wads in a wastebasket. And a hitter doesn't fatten a batting average by swatting flies off the dinner table.

No, sir. It won't happen. The only way to improve your fielding, throwing, and hitting is to field, throw, and hit. Here are eight suggestions to guide you:

● Practice alone or practice with a few friends.

● Practice with your team. Be on time—people count on you.

● If you want to really improve, combine the two previous suggestions.

● Stay busy.

● Have fun. Enjoy what you're doing.

● If you need extra work on fielding ground balls, ask somebody to hit you plenty of grounders. Go left, go right, just keep going.

● Pace yourself, take it easy, and keep things simple.

● If you face a problem, ask for help. Don't be bashful. You won't improve unless you make an effort.

What Can You Expect from Practice Games?

Action. Plenty of action. And a chance to try something new, like a heavier bat or bigger glove. That's what you can expect from practice games.

Maybe you'd like to play first base instead of third. Okay, go to first base and see what happens. After two or three games, you'll know where you stand. Yes, indeed. Practice games have a way of squeezing out the truth.

The long layoff between seasons causes bones to rust and muscles to tighten. If you move too fast, your body may never forgive you. Thank God for practice games. They act as a lubricant and get you loose for the upcoming season.

A word of caution: don't go overboard. Sure, you're anxious to play. But let those cold, dormant muscles wake up gradually. Start the season fresh, free from the pain of strain.

Don't Let the Weather Beat You

A cold windy day kills the desire to play catch and snuffs the life out of swinging a bat.

Plans change quickly in the early spring. You wake up in the morning feeling good, really wanting to smack a ball. Then you hear the howling wind telling you to go back to bed. Stick cotton in your ears. Tell the wind to breeze off. You're going to take hitting practice in the garage.

Garage? Yes, garage. It sounds a bit crazy, but here's what you do. Cut out a paper or cardboard circle the size of a softball. Tape it on the inside of your garage door. Make sure the circle is at least 3 feet off the ground.

Pick up a bat and stand about 5 feet away from the door. Picture in your mind a pitcher throwing a ball. Pretend the circle is a pitch coming at you. Now swing at the ball. Think about hitting the ball back at the pitcher. Swing the bat for 5 or 10 minutes. Start out with a slow, easy swing. When you feel your body muscles loosen, swing a little harder. If you begin to tire, quit. You'll have plenty of time to practice.

Don't let cold, windy or wet weather stop you—stay inside. Do stretching exercises, swing a bat, jump rope, chin yourself from the garage rafters—do anything that helps you prepare your mind and body for playing slow pitch.

How Does the Schedule Look?

A swell way to gain enemies and bomb out before the season starts is to sign up for a team, wait until a day after the signup deadline, then quit. Heck, it's not your fault. You've been going to Aunt Mabel's house for chicken dinner every Tuesday night for the last five years. Who made up the stupid schedule anyway? Any dope knows Tuesday night is a lousy time to play ball.

Don't, please don't, pull an Aunt Mabel. Sponsors yell. Managers rip buttons from their shirts. Team players run for the bat rack. You'll need police protection to arrive home safely.

Ah, but you can avoid all of this heartache. Simply find out game days and times before signing up for a team. Plan to show up ready to play. You might miss a game or two—most players do. No one will nail your shoes to the wall. At least you'll be able to tell the manager ahead of time.

Putting It All Together

It's time to play ball and you've never been more anxious. You've shined your shoes, oiled your glove, and hugged your bat. You've seen the game schedule and it looks good.

This will be an exciting season for you. You plan to work hard, have fun, and practice often. Cold weather won't stop you. You came to play and here you are. You respect your friends and yourself. You're not going to charge the field like a bull chasing a matador. No, you plan to bring your body around gradually, limbering up your arms and legs as you go.

Who could ask for anything more?

Stepping Up to the Plate

Getting Ready to Swing

Think back for a moment. When was the last time you swung a bat? Six months ago? Eight months ago? A player who foolishly tries to kill the ball early in the season makes a big mistake. Idle muscles need time to respond. Give your muscles a chance to come around. Don't let a quick swing of the bat keep you out of action.

Loosen Those Stiff Muscles

Swing a bat daily for five or ten minutes, beginning two or three weeks before the season gets under way. Start by bringing the bat around slow and easy. Repeat several times while concentrating on fully extending the bat until you feel the forearm and shoulder muscles begin to stretch out.

Now swing a little harder. Let the wrists and hips rotate in unison as the bat sweeps forward. Bring the bat around with a complete follow-through motion.

Before you take batting practice, try these three simple exercises:

EXERCISE 5 (Illus. 5)

1. Pick up a bat. Wrap your right hand around the heavy end and your left hand around the handle. Stand erect with feet spread shoulder-width apart.

2. Keep arms and legs straight. Slowly lower the bat toward your toes. Take your time. Stretch as far as you can, but be careful not to strain yourself.

3. Return to original position. Relax your body.

4. Repeat four or five times.

Illus. 5.   **Illus. 6.**

EXERCISE 6 (Illus. 6)

1. Assume the position described in Exercise 5.

2. Keep your arms and legs straight. Raise the bat high over your head, rise up on your toes, and lean back as far as possible. Hold this position for approximately 5 seconds.

3. Return to original position and relax.

4. Repeat four or five times.

EXERCISE 7 (Illus. 7)

1. Lay a bat on the ground. Stand in front of it with your feet spread shoulder-width apart. Place the heel of your right foot next to the heavy end of the bat and the heel of your left foot next to the handle.

2. Slowly reach down and grab the middle of the bat with both hands. Try to keep both legs straight.

3. Lift the bat behind your legs to a point halfway between knees and buttocks.

Illus. 7. Keep arms straight, lean back and pull hard on the bat. Hold this position for about five seconds.

4. Return the bat to its original position and relax.

5. Repeat four or five times.

Stay loose by taking three or four good cuts. Keep in mind that a strong wrist snap will bring the bat around faster.

Scanning the Bat Rack

Now it's time to select a bat that's right for you. Baseball bats, like automobiles, come in different sizes, colors and shapes. Some players like aluminum bats, others prefer solid wood. Picking a bat is analogous to buying a car. Few people walk into a car showroom and buy the first one they see. Likewise, a smart player will shop around before making a final choice.

TRY THEM ONE AT A TIME

Go to the bat rack. Pick up each bat one at a time. Take two or three swings at an imaginary ball. Then make two separate stacks. Discard those bats which feel awkward—too heavy, too light, too long or too short. Keep only those bats which give you a smooth, easy swing. If you have a tough time deciding, try this simple test. Have another player pitch to you. Swing at several pitches with each selected bat. After each pitch, ask yourself, "Did the bat take my mind off the ball?" If it did, find another bat and continue to swing. You'll soon find the right bat.

It has been said that bat selection is psychological. A good athlete can hit with practically any bat. Don't you believe it! A bat that raises doubts also lowers the batting average.

Protect Your Selection

When you make a final choice, your responsibility begins. Stay alert; many things happen to a wayward bat. Here are a few bat-saving suggestions:

● The rack is for the bat. A player may seriously injure an ankle by stepping on a bat left lying around, and cleat marks do little to enhance the value or beauty of a bat.

● Keep fresh tape on the handle. This improves the grip and makes the bat more attractive. This is, though, a matter of personal preference. Some players prefer aluminum bats with rubber-coated handles or wooden bats with smooth, untaped handles.

● Don't throw the bat against the backstop or metal sideline fence. Never take your anger out on the bat. After all, the bat is only following directions.

● Make it a point to know where your bat is at all times. Losing your favorite bat is almost as bad as misplacing your car keys.

● If possible, keep the bat in your possession. Take it home after every game. Hide it in your closet. You'll sleep better.

How to Pick the Right Grip

A successful batter knows that a firm but relaxed grip that allows the wrists to rotate freely is the key to consistent hitting. How can you find a grip that's right for you? Let's examine the techniques some choke hitters and power hitters use.

CHOKE UP A BIT

A choke hitter holds both hands close together a few inches up the bat handle (Illus. 8). A choke grip cuts down on power, but gives the player better bat control.

Illus. 8 (left). Choking up.

Illus. 9 (above). Line up of middle knuckles of both hands to keep wrists loose.

Pick up your favorite bat, assume a choke grip and take two or three swings. How does it feel? If your wrists seem tight, line up the middle knuckles of both hands (Illus. 9). This grip allows the wrists to rotate freely when the bat crosses in front of your body.

Don't let a first impression fool you—test your swing against live pitching. Find a pitching partner, go to a field and step up to the plate. Before the first pitch, bring the bat slowly across home plate. Notice how the wrists turn as the bat sweeps forward. Now hit seven or eight pitches. Fix your eyes on the ball. Concentrate on making solid contact with the pitch out in front of home plate.

SWING WITH POWER

An athlete who prefers to swing hard and drive the ball a long distance seldom uses a choke grip. As a rule, power hitters hold their hands low, touching or covering the knob of the bat, although a few choose to choke up slightly on the bat. They may either line up the middle knuckles of both hands or line up the middle knuckles of the top hand somewhere between the large knuckles and middle knuckles of the bottom hand (Illus. 10a and b).

A choke hitter tries to punch or slap the ball over an infielder's head. Conversely, a power hitter employs a strong, whip-like thrust of the

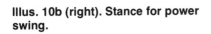

Illus. 10a (above). Grip for power swing.

Illus. 10b (right). Stance for power swing.

bat to make solid contact with the ball. Not everyone is big enough or strong enough to hit for distance. If you have the ability to spray hits around the field, forget the long ball. Those punch singles fatten the batting average and produce runs.

Take a Comfortable Stance

The next step to successful hitting is to find a comfortable stance. Don't make the mistake of copying another player's batting style. It just won't work. Hitting is an individual matter which requires study, determination and long hours of practice.

Take your time. As you approach home plate, let your feet find a natural path in the batter's box. Rock back and forth until your body rests comfortably over both feet. When everything feels right, touch the outside corner of home plate with the fat end of the bat. If you have trouble reaching the corner, move closer to the plate. Be sure your bat covers home plate completely.

Experiment with the following three stances and find one that suits you best.

STRAIGHTAWAY STANCE (Illus. 11)

● Step up to home plate. Spread your feet apart until your body rests comfortably over them.

● Bend slightly at the knees and shift your body weight to the rear foot.

● Keep your feet parallel to one another.

OPEN STANCE (Illus. 12)

● Step up to home plate. Spread your feet apart until your body rests comfortably over them.

● Bend slightly at the knees and shift your weight to the rear foot.

● Move your front foot (the one closest to the pitcher) away from the plate.

CLOSED STANCE (Illus. 13)

● Step up to home plate. Spread your feet apart until your weight rests comfortably over them.

● Bend slightly at the knees and shift your weight to the rear foot.

● Move front foot (the one closest to pitcher) toward home plate.

Testing Your Stance and Swing

Let's find out if your stance and swing will produce satisfying results. Have your pitching partner throw to you. Work on the following techniques:

● Relax hands, wrists and forearms.

● Hold elbows away from your body and extend the bat back toward the catcher.

● Keep your head still and fix your eyes on the ball.

● As the pitcher releases the ball, take a short step forward, bring the bat around, shift your weight from your rear foot to your front foot and follow through completely. Try to hit the ball when your weight, moving from back foot to front foot, is evenly balanced over both feet. A good follow-through allows the bat to carry beyond the side of the body facing the pitcher.

**Illus. 11.
Straightaway
stance.**

**Illus. 12. Open
stance.**

**Illus. 13. Closed
stance.**

● Keep bat extended to assure complete plate coverage.

Note: Slow pitch rules prohibit chopping down on the ball. Many players, especially power hitters, swing in an upward direction to lift the ball high into the air. Most punch hitters use a level swing, parallel to the ground.

What kind of hitter do you want to become? Should you be a punch hitter or power hitter? Should you alternate between punching the ball and hitting for distance? After a game or two, you'll discover how effective you are with the bat.

Let's say you want to hit for a high average and reach base often. Fine. Punch hitting is for you. You'll have to work hard to develop excellent bat control and perfect timing. The next section will start you on your way.

Tips for the Punch Hitter

Here are some guidelines to help you punch your way on base:

● Choke up an inch or two on the bat handle.

● Relax your entire body. Many players believe that taking one or two deep breaths helps them relax.

● Study the defense. Look for pockets or holes between the outfielders.

● Pick a good pitch. For example, let's say the left fielder, playing toward center field, leaves the line open. A smart right-handed batter will hit an inside pitch down the line. Conversely, a left-handed hitter will wait for an outside pitch.

● Wait on the pitch. Let it reach home plate before taking a short step in the direction you want to hit. Avoid leaning or reaching for the ball.

● Bring the bat around making sure your hands and arms remain out in front of your body. Drive the ball forward with a quick wrist snap and a complete follow-through of the bat.

The best way to become a top punch hitter is to develop perfect timing through constant practice. Set aside time during the week to refine your swing. Strengthen the arm, back, and shoulder muscles through daily exercise.

Illus. 14 and 15. These two punch-hitting stances, as well as other variations, can be used successfully. Find the one that's right for you.

Tips for the Power Hitter

As mentioned earlier, most power hitters hold the bat low on the handle and swing hard. Relaxation, concentration and strong wrists make up part of the power package. The following suggestions will help you hit with power:

● Check wind conditions by throwing grass or small pieces of paper in the air. A strong wind blowing hard toward home plate creates problems for the power hitter.

● Look for open areas in the outfield. Notice if the outfielders are playing deep or shallow.

● Use a grip that allows the wrists to roll in an easy, comfortable fashion. This rolling effect generates power to drive the ball deep into the outfield. Try to time the swing so wrists, shoulders and hips rotate when the bat meets the ball. Bring the bat around with a complete follow-through motion.

● Take a wide stance in the batter's box, that is, bring the lead foot 5 or 6 inches closer to the pitcher. This opens the hips and adds power to the swing.

● You can increase bat speed by rocking back on your rear foot, lifting the lead foot and whipping the bat around quickly.

● Don't overstride (move your lead foot too far forward during your swing). A batter who overstrides throws his timing off and swing under the pitch, causing the ball to pop up.

● Remember—there is no substitute for hard practice.

How to Improve as a Hitter

Nearly every batter, regardless of hitting style, wants to make solid contact with the ball. Few athletes enjoy walking back to the bench muttering, "Another lousy pop-up. Why didn't I clobber the ball?"

Look over the following ideas. Think about them. Practice them. And use them to help you improve.

APPROACH HOME PLATE WITH CONFIDENCE

There's an old baseball saying: A batter who swings is dangerous. Keep this philosophy in mind. As long as you can swing the bat, you have an excellent chance of hitting the ball.

Some players let a ground ball hit weakly onto the infield or a sky high pop-up ruin their confidence. Nobody hits every pitch hard. Nobody. A player who is determined simply to make solid contact with the ball poses a constant threat to the defense.

STAY IN THE GAME

Be a thinker. As you approach home plate, ask yourself the following questions: What is the score? How many outs are there? What inning is it? Where would be the best place to hit the ball? And so on.

Physical conditions dictate strategy. In other words, a power hitter would be smart to punch the ball when outfielders are playing deep or when the wind is blowing hard toward home plate. A stubborn player who refuses to adjust does little to help his or her team win softball games.

LOOK THE BALL OVER

Take a strike. Watch the ball carefully. Notice how the pitcher grips the ball. Does the ball spin backward or forward? Does the ball have a side spin or slow spin? (These pitches are described in *When You Take the Mound.*)

Illus. 16 and 17. When you swing with power, you'll naturally take a longer follow-through than a punch hitter. Just remember not to overswing, that is, swing with more power than you can control.

Observe how the pitcher delivers the ball. Does it travel through a high arc or low arc? Does the hurler keep the ball inside or outside? Study the pitcher throughout the game. An intelligent hurler knows how to spot pitch, that is, move the ball around the strike zone.

The hardest thing for a batter to do is wait on a pitch. An average, high-arc pitch takes about two seconds to reach home plate. Don't be in a hurry. Wait for your pitch and give it a ride.

TWO STRIKES. NOW WHAT?

You get only three strikes in slow pitch. You can't afford to be selective with two strikes on you. If you miss the ball again, you're out. Make up your mind to swing at any pitch around the plate. Go with the pitch. Hit inside pitches down the line and outside pitches into the opposite field.

KNOW THE STRIKE ZONE

Don't help the pitcher by swinging at bad pitches. Hit only strikes. Slow pitch rules say a ball must be delivered at a height of at least 3 feet, but not over 10 feet, before reaching home plate. A strike is any ball which crosses home plate between a batter's shoulders and knees. But not all umpires call pitches the same way. Talk to the umpire before the game. Find out his interpretation of the strike zone and adjust your stance accordingly.

IT'S ALL IN THE WRISTS

Spend time building up your wrist, finger, and forearm muscles. Alternate squeezing a rubber ball, tennis ball or hunk of clay with each hand. If you can't find a ball, make a fist, squeeze tight, hold for 5 seconds and release.

Repeat this exercise as often as possible.

Putting It All Together

Keep muscles loose and ready for action. Take plenty of batting practice and work on perfecting the swing. Assume a comfortable stance and use a grip that allows the wrists to roll freely. Study your opposition. Stay alert, believe in yourself and know what is happening at all times during the game.

Traveling Around the Bases

Forget what Lou Brock says about stealing bases. (You can't steal in slow pitch.)

Forget what Maury Wills suggests about taking a big lead. (You can't lead off base in slow pitch.)

With so much to forget, you're probably wondering what there is that's worth remembering about base running.

Well, don't be discouraged. You can still slide into bases and tag up on fly balls. And the athlete who thrives on stretching singles into doubles makes base running an exciting part of the game. So let's turn our attention to base running and find out how to score runs.

Beating the Throw to First

A hustling player often turns a slow bouncing ball into a base hit. That's a simple, direct statement. But sadly, the word "hustle" holds little meaning to some athletes. Since you're not the type to give up easily, the following suggestions will help you beat the throw to first base.

● After the swing, explode out of the batter's box. Shove off with your left foot, then take a step with your right foot (if you're a right-handed hitter). Continue to run in a straight path down the baseline. Conversely, a left-handed hitter takes off with the right foot, then steps forward with the left foot.

● Look straight ahead. Focus your eyes on first base. Avoid watching the ball—unnecessary head movement will slow you down.

● Run with short, choppy steps.

● Hit the bag with either foot.

● Don't change stride or jump for the bag at the last minute. A quick step cuts speed, throws off timing, and may cause you to trip over the base.

● After touching the bag, continue to run several feet past it, then slow down gradually.

To practice your getaway from home plate, bring a friend, a bat, and a stop watch to a softball diamond. Prior to the drill, loosen up by doing some bending and stretching exercises. Jog around the base path four or five times. Then sprint around twice.

Send your friend to the first base coach's box to time you. Go to home plate, swing at an imaginary pitch, explode from the batter's box, and sprint to first base. Have your friend start timing when you complete the swing.

Repeat four or five times. Average your time by dividing the number of attempts into the total time.

Check your progress periodically. If your time doesn't improve, have someone check your start or getaway from home plate.

Rounding First Base

An alert runner takes an extra base when an infielder lets the ball go through or when an outfielder fumbles the ball. What is a good way to round first base and reach second? Try these time-saving techniques:

● While running to first, watch to see if a fielder misplays the ball. Pay attention to the first base coach.

● If a fielder bobbles the ball, start to round first base by swinging out to the right of the baseline to begin an arc that will bring you to the inside of first base.

● Circle the base at full speed, lean your weight toward second base, and hit the inside corner of the bag with either foot.

● Shove off hard from first base and sprint toward second. *Important:* Don't break stride.

Work on circling first base. Place two bases in a straight line about 60 feet apart. (A folded canvas bag makes a suitable base.) Take a batting stance next to Bag One (home plate). Swing at an imaginary ball, sprint toward Bag Two (first base), and circle it.

Illus. 18 (left). Practice your getaway from home plate.

Illus. 19 (right). Be prepared to round first base and go on to second if the fielder bobbles the ball.

Now run in the opposite direction. Go to Bag Two, assume a batting stance, and repeat the procedure. Continue the drill until you can hit the inside of the bag with either foot without breaking your stride.

Stretching a Single into a Double

Would you like to reach second base on every single you hit?

Unfortunately, you can't. It won't happen. Nobody is that fast. But you can improve your chances of taking an extra base if you consider the following points.

First, get to know the opposition. Watch the outfielders throw during pre-game warm ups. Find out which players have strong arms and where these athletes play in the outfield. Let's say a right-handed, poor-throwing athlete is playing center field. Try to punch a base hit to the fielder's non-throwing (left) side. If you succeed, head for second, and slide into the base. Bear in mind that the player has a weak arm and is out of position to make a good throw.

Second, bait an outfielder into making a quick throw to second base. After hitting a long single into the outfield, pour on the speed, round

Illus. 22. Hit first base with either foot and keep going.

Illus. 21. Swing your weight inward toward the diamond as you approach first base.

Illus. 20. Start out expecting to round first base and stretch a single into a double.

first, and run hard for second. Keep running until the fielder throws the ball. Then stop between first and second, keep your eyes on the ball, and be ready to hurry back to first. If the ball is mishandled or overthrown, take second and slide into the base. If the throw is on target, return to first. But stay awake. A heady outfielder might throw behind you, that is, fake to second and fire the ball to first base. A confused outfielder often holds onto the ball and runs toward the infield. Play it safe. Return to first and stay there.

A wise runner takes an extra base when an outfielder stays deep, leaves a gap in the outfield, reacts slowly to the ball, or is in a non-throwing position. One final point—never take a chance when your team can't spare an out.

From First to Second

A runner in slow pitch would have to be a magician to shake up the pitcher. Since a player isn't allowed to lead off or steal, the hurler can concentrate on pitching to the batter. Does this mean a runner can relax and wait for the batter to hit the ball? Maybe, but a smart runner will try to get a good jump to the next base. Here are two methods which will give you a fast start:

Illus. 23. Method 1: Face the batter and rest your left foot against first base. When the ball is hit, pivot on your right foot and head for second base.

METHOD 1: FACE THE BATTER

● Stand next to first base, face the batter, and rest your left foot against the inside corner of the bag.

● Keep your feet spread shoulder-width apart. Bring your weight slightly forward, extend your arms out in front of your body, bend at the knees, and make a quarter turn to the right.

● When the batter hits the ball, pivot on your right foot, throw your left foot across your right leg, and run hard for second base.

METHOD 2: TURN TOWARD SECOND

● Stand next to first base and watch the batter. Step on the inside corner of the bag with either foot. Turn your body toward second base.

● Bring your weight slightly forward, extend your arms out in front of you, and bend at the knees.

● When the batter hits the ball, push off hard from the base and sprint for second.

Don't get doubled off base—be ready to dive back into first base if an infielder catches a line drive. Also, go halfway on a fly ball hit medium deep to the outfield.

Illus. 24. Method 2: Turn toward second while keeping your left foot on first base. When the ball is hit push off hard and sprint for second base.

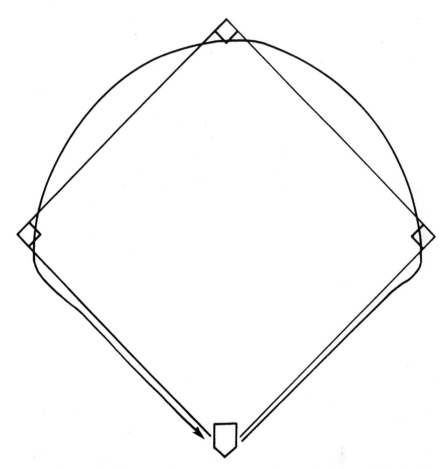

Illus. 25. Getting around the bases fastest requires you to lose as little speed as possible turning the corners.

The Fastest Way Around

It's always a thrill to hit a ball hard and drive it deep into the outfield. A ball that rolls between two outfielders almost guarantees the batter an extra-base hit. Let's pretend you've hit a ball deep between the center fielder and right fielder. Would you like to get around the bases in a hurry? OK, here we go:

● Get a good jump out of the batter's box and turn on the speed.

● When you near first base, begin a turn that will allow you to hit the inside corner of the base with either foot. Push off hard, lean your weight toward second base, and run in a slight arc around second and third. Touch the inside corner of each.

● Keep your eyes and ears open. Let the base coaches direct you.

Here's a practice tip: Arrive at the park early. Step up to home plate, swing at an imaginary ball, and run at half speed around the bases. Do this twice. Repeat the procedure, running twice around the bases at full speed.

Have someone clock you and keep a record of your times. If you seem to be slowing down, check for these faults:

● Slow start out of the batter's box.

● Beginning circle too late.

● Circling too wide.

● Breaking stride.

● Not leaning weight toward the infield.

Tag Up and Go!

Tagging up on fly balls to the outfield not only advances the runner but makes base running fun. A close play at the bag brings a moment of excitement for both player and fan. Remember these points the next time you tag up on a fly ball:

● Make sure the ball travels high and deep into the outfield.

● Set yourself for a fast take-off from the base. Use any method that will let you fire out.

● Push hard from the base at the exact moment the fielder catches the ball. If you can't see well enough to decide, stay on base. Work with the base coach. Listen for the coach to shout "Go."

● After you leave the bag, keep your eyes fixed on the base ahead.

● Notice how the infielder covers the bag. If it looks like a close play, stay low and slide hard.

Here is a good rule to keep in mind: Never tag up unless you get a good jump and believe you can beat the throw. Trying to outrun a bullet throw from shallow outfield is like running up a steep hill covered with ice. After the first few steps, you know it's hopeless.

Down and Dirty

Athletes slide to avoid a baseman's tag or to keep from going past the base. A player who knows how to slide is an asset to the team.

Before discussing how to slide, look over these important points:

● Protect yourself against slide burns or strawberries by wearing long pants and sliding pads. A strawberry appears when the outer layer of skin comes off leaving a sticky, oozing surface.

● Inspect the infield turf, especially around the bases, before game-time. An experienced player knows that a hard infield can scrape off skin like a dull razor blade.

● If you think sliding is too dangerous, go into the base standing up. But be fair to your team—don't try for an extra base unless you're ready to slide.

● Once you decide to slide, don't change your mind. A last-minute decision can put you out of action. Nobody likes to sit on the bench nursing a pulled muscle, twisted ankle, or broken leg.

Now let's work on the fundamentals of sliding.

Be Direct!

There's nothing fancy about a come-ahead or straight-on slide. A runner has one objective in mind—to get to the base as fast as possible. A straight-on slide carries the runner directly into the bag. Take a look at the following techniques:

● Run straight at the bag.

● Begin the slide about 8 to 10 feet from the bag. Be careful—the take-off point is a critical part of sliding and differs with each athlete. Injuries occur when players leave their feet too soon or too late.

● Use either foot for take-off. Keep the opposite leg extended straight ahead and high off the ground.

● Once in the air, lean the upper part of your body backwards and bend the take-off leg under the extended leg. Keep the bent leg turned sideways to prevent spikes from digging into the ground.

● Slide on the bent-leg side. Use the leg and buttocks to cushion the fall.

● Use the extended leg to touch the near side of the bag and bring yourself back up to a standing position.

Use the Hook!

Many players hook-slide into base to avoid being tagged out by a fielder. An evasive hook slide carries the body to the opposite side of a fielder's tag. Let's suppose you're heading for second base and the baseman, standing to the right of the bag, is about to receive the ball. What should you do? Test the infielder's skill by hook-sliding to the left or infield side of the base.

Follow this procedure:

● Run straight at the bag.

● Begin the slide about 8 to 10 feet from bag.

● Leave ground with the left foot, bend both knees to the side, lean the upper part of your body backwards, and shift your weight to the left side.

Illus. 26. The straight-on or come-ahead slide has one objective—to get to the base as fast as possible.

Illus. 27. The hook slide carries you away from the baseman's tag.

● Slide directly into the bag. Hook the near corner of the bag with your right foot.

● Hold your hands and elbows up and out of the way.

● If you must hook-slide to the right, leave the ground with your right foot, turn your body to that side, and hook the bag with your left foot.

Don't wait until game-time to practice sliding. Bring a glove and two bases (towels or canvas bags) to a grassy field. Be sure to wear socks, long pants, and sliding pads. Leave your spikes at home. (Never wear spikes while practicing sliding. You may hurt an ankle or leg.)

Try these sliding drills:

DRILL 1: BACK AND FORTH

1. Set two bases 60 feet apart in a straight line.

2. Assume a standing position next to Base One. Break toward Base Two and hook-slide to the left of the bag.

3. Come to your feet. Take a standing position next to Base Two. Break toward Base One and hook-slide to the right of the bag.

4. Repeat this procedure five or six times.

DRILL 2: STRAIGHT-ON AND HOOK

1. Set two bases 60 feet apart in a straight line.

2. Stand next to Base One. Place a glove along the left side of the base. Break toward Base Two and come into the bag with a straight-on slide.

3. Come to your feet. Take a standing position next to Base Two. Break toward Base One and hook-slide to the opposite side of the glove.

4. Repeat this procedure five or six times.

Listen to the Base Coaches

Don't run the bases alone. Let the base coaches assist you around the base paths. And when it's your turn to coach the bases, accept the challenge. Some players think a base coach is nothing more than a field ornament. This poor attitude is detrimental to team morale. A base coach, interested in winning games, is the best friend a base runner can have.

The first base coach is responsible for advising the runner on first base regarding:

● Number of outs and the score.

● Where infielders and outfielders are playing.

● When to tag up on fly balls.

● Watching for line drives in the infield with less than two outs.

● Overrunning a base or passing another runner.

● Touching all of the bases.

A third base coach uses voice and hand signals to direct a runner where to slide (left or right), to hold up runners, and to wave them around third base. He also keeps the runners on second and third posted on the number of outs, score, when to tag up, and base-running strategy for various situations.

Putting It All Together

A base runner should have fair speed, be alert, and be ready to take an extra base. He should listen to and follow directions given by the base coaches. An intelligent base runner finds time to practice the correct methods of base running, sliding, and how to fire out of the batter's box.

Putting Runs on the Scoreboard

If you want to win, outscore the other team. How do you outscore the other team? By getting more runs. And how do you get more runs? Keep reading. You'll see.

How to Build a Strong Batting Order

If you want to crush every team in the league, find ten power hitters capable of knocking the seams off the ball. There. See how simple it is? Now you have a batting order every manager drools over. Impossible? Not in open class competition, but in recreational slow pitch, highly unlikely.

Let's suppose you're a team manager and you want a strong, run-producing batting order. How would you go about getting one?

First, hold three or four pre-season batting practice sessions. Watch your players swing away. Notice how each player hits the ball. Also keep track of the fast runners. Take good mental notes. If you have a poor memory, write down what you see.

Second, categorize players, that is, put each player in a separate group. Here are five examples:

● Slugger, slow to average speed. (Speed is not a large factor.)

● Slugger, fast runner. (Again, speed is not critical if the batter hits with power.)

● Line-drive hitter, fair power, average to good speed.

● Combination slugger and line-drive hitter, average speed.

● Puncher, fair to good speed.

Now scan your notes and come up with a super lineup. Remember, you're after runs, gobs of runs. Take your punch or line-drive hitters and stick them ahead of the sluggers. If everything goes right, the punchers will hit singles or doubles and the sluggers will sweep the bases with home runs (according to batting-order theory, that is). In other words, your team should stay at bat until the balls wear out, disappear, or turn into dust.

Nice idea. But batters get blisters on their hands when they hit for long periods of time. Besides, nobody bats a thousand—not even players in open class competition. There's always a "rally killer" who pops up or grounds out.

Maybe you can't bribe a power hitter to play for your team. So what? You can still win your share of games. Just find ten players who reach base most of the time, aren't afraid to hustle, and enjoy each other's company.

Who's Got the Rocket?

It's downright embarrassing. You look for a base to hide under. There's really very little you can say.

Confused? Okay, here's the situation: You come to bat, swing at your favorite pitch, and paste it between left and center fields. You round first and trot toward second base. An automatic stand-up double, or so you think.

Then it happens. A bullet throw stings the second baseman's glove. The baseman, in turn, spins around and spears your shin with a tag.

You're out! You didn't even slide. Do you feel your face turning red? It should. You made a big, big mistake. You never bothered to check which defensive players carry the shotgun arms. You didn't seek out the rockets, those cannon arms which can cut you down faster than a wood cutter's axe. Shame, shame on you.

Close plays are exciting. It's fun to go for an extra base. It shows you're a heads up, hustling, energetic player. However, think of your team. Never risk an out when:

● Your team can't afford one.

● Your team trails by several runs, and one more run will have little meaning at this point in the game.

- Your chance of beating the throw is very slim.

- You do not plan to slide.

When you play a team for the first time, study how each outfielder throws. Pay special attention to these four points:

- Ball speed.

- Throwing accuracy.

- Speed afoot.

- Quickness in getting rid of the ball.

This information increases your chances of staying alive on the bases. You'll know whom you can run on and whom you can't. But a word of caution is in order—be sure that you evaluate your opposition on the basis of how they play, not on how you think they *look like* they'll play.

It's not unusual to see a player running around in cut-offs or long-legged pants. Few sponsors can afford bats, balls, entry fees, and complete uniforms for every player on the team.

There's an old saying, "Clothes don't make the man." Well, here's a modern one: "A uniform doesn't tell you anything about a player's ability." Translation: Ragged looking players swing bats, hit home runs, and sprint as fast as fully uniformed players.

Yes, they do. So show good sense. Respect stained shirts and torn pants. They may be worn by the player who'll throw you out at home plate. And you don't win many games being on the north end of an umpire's thumb.

Watch That Relay

Once you spot the rocket arms, the next step is to see how well the infield and outfield work together on relay throws.

Situation: Nobody on base. You hit a line-drive base hit into left field. The shortstop moves into shallow left, takes the relay throw, and tosses it to the second baseman. A very routine play.

However, when an outfielder with slow reactions teams up with a lazy infielder, a routine play may turn into a real laugher. Well, you get the last chuckle. Go for the extra base. An opportunity like this doesn't come around every game. Become a magician on the bases. Turn a single into a stand-up double. Your manager will spin cartwheels and the fans will wad up hot-dog wrappers and throw them at one another.

But be careful. Don't get carried away. Few teams can afford to let a situation like this go on for very long. So don't get the idea you'll beat every relay throw.

While your team's at bat, study the defense. Watch. Observe. Separate the lazy, slow-moving players from the hustlers with strong, accurate arms. Remember—the razor with the sharpest edge cuts deeper. Or stated another way, the hustling team, in the long run, scores more runs.

Keep Your Eye on the Rover

A rover, or second short fielder, creeps around like an alley cat after scraps of food. A clever rover knows where to play and can wipe out a rally before it erupts.

Here's an example: You punch the ball and most everything you hit goes up the middle of the diamond. A rover, knowing your hitting style, will play somewhere between second base and center field. Defensive strategy. That's what it is. And unless you can adjust, your batting average will dive faster than a pelican after an anchovy.

A smart hitter watches where the defense plays, especially the rover, and adjusts accordingly. For instance, if you're a slugger and the rover plays deep (open field, no fence) with the other three outfielders, punch the ball in front of them—go for a base hit instead of a homer. If you're stubborn and refuse to cut down on your swing, don't expect to be much help to your team.

There's a simple answer. If the rover plays deep, hit short. If the rover plays in left field, go up the middle or into right field. And if you find the rover lurking about in shallow center, poke the ball into left or right field. In short, if the rover's here, go over there.

Advice costs nothing. Sure, it's easier said than done. So practice spray hitting. Work on punching the ball into the opposite field, down the line, up the middle, or any place you don't see the rover hiding.

Don't Let the Pitcher Fool You

We've said it's nearly impossible for a pitcher to fool you in slow pitch. Yet some pitchers manage to drive you crazy by mixing their pitches, tossing high and low, inside and outside, or whatever. First, you see a backspin. Then maybe a finger ball or knuckle ball wiggles up to the plate. Then, who knows? A creative pitcher keeps things interesting. It's almost worth coming to bat just to see what the pitcher plans to throw you.

All in all, you're in the driver's seat. You know a pitcher must throw slowly and keep the ball between 3 feet and 10 feet above the ground. So here come the batting tips of the century. Read them carefully. Follow them religiously. Do this and your team manager will love you to death.

● When you're at bat, have patience. Wait. If necessary, take one or two strikes before swinging at the ball. Don't swing at anything but *your* pitch. Relax. Your pitch will come. Wait and see.

● Watch the ball from the time it leaves the pitcher's hand until it lands in the catcher's glove. Get your timing down by mentally swinging at the ball. Picture in your mind the exact time you'd whip the bat around. Then when you decide to swing, you'll have a better chance to hit the ball solidly.

As an example, nearly every player on Campbell's Carpets, 1978 ASA National Slow Pitch Champs, follows the pitch in this manner. Even the guys who hit two or more home runs a game keep their eyes glued on the ball as it crosses home plate.

● Concentrate on hitting the ball out in front of home plate with the fat end of the bat. Try to make contact when body weight shifts from rear foot to front foot. (In the case of a right-handed hitter, weight would shift from right foot to left foot.)

You know that the best way to become a successful hitter is to practice hitting.

So go hit.

Putting It All Together

As a team manager, you'll juggle your lineup to give your team power, punch, and runs.

As a player, you'll stay extra sharp and study the opposing team. You'll find out who can throw and who can't. And you'll be able to separate the slowpokes from the sprinters.

Don't be a stubborn hitter. If an outfielder plays you three miles deep or a strong wind blows into your face, cut down on your swing. Go for a base hit. After all, a long, high fly ball caught near the fence is nothing more than a long, high out. So save the big swing for another game.

Practice time approaches. Work on bat control. Stress punching the ball into the open spaces.

How to Play the Infield

Would you rather field a ground ball than find a fifty-dollar bill? Would you rather catch a high pop fly than eat a barbecued steak? If you answer yes to these two questions, you're either rich or a vegetarian or both.

But maybe you're not rich and you like steak more than any other food. Then what? Then play the infield. All the signs are in your favor.

What Are the Physical Requirements?

Nothing special. Just about anyone can play somewhere in the infield. You can be fast or slow, tall or short, stocky or thin, male or female, young or old. What skills do you need to be a good, solid infielder?

First, the ability to make accurate underhand, sidearm, and overhand throws. Second, the ability to bend over and stay low while fielding ground balls. Third, the ability to go left, right, forward, or backward on a line drive or fly ball.

Let's back up for a second. We said nearly anyone can play somewhere in the infield. The key word is somewhere. For example, a big, slow-moving player would make a far better catcher than shortstop; a player with fair speed and an average arm would be better off playing second than shortstop, and so on.

If you have your heart set on playing a certain position, say first base, play it. So maybe you're shorter than most first basemen. So what? Size didn't stop Napoleon. Work hard. Do whatever it takes to help you improve your fielding. Don't worry about your height. Let your glove make up the difference.

What Are the Mental Requirements?

Playing the infield is like studying for a test. The more you apply yourself, the better the results. The same thing goes for brain power. If you want to be a successful infielder, you must learn early to stay alert, think ahead, and anticipate what will happen next.

Anticipation, or knowing what to expect, is part of the mental package. You don't need an old gypsy lady with a crystal ball to keep you one step ahead of your opponent. For example, the fourth batter in the lineup steps to the plate. He's big, really big. Looks mean enough to lick postage stamps with his breath. You're playing third base. And you know he'll be swinging from his shoes. Where will you play? If you're wise, as far back as good sense allows.

One last point—don't play the infield unless you love to field ground balls. If ground balls force you to close your eyes and turn your head, say hello to the outfield.

Keep Low to the Ground

Sing. Hum. Whistle. Curl your tongue. Do anything you want, but stay low. And never, never let a ground ball sneak under your glove.

Illus. 28 and 29. Position for fielding ground balls for best balance. Left, front view; right, side view.

Illus. 30. Keep your eyes glued to the ball until it is safely in your glove.

Illus. 28 and 29 show a low body stance for fielding ground balls. Here are the main points:

● Bend at the knees and hips. Keep your weight forward, up over the balls of your feet. Touch your glove to the ground. This forces your tail end to drop closer to the ground.

● Keep your legs spread shoulder-width apart to help your balance.

● Extend your arms out in front of your body. Point your elbows to the side, turn your palms inward, and hold your fingers together.

● Keep your eyes glued to the ball.

● Look the ball into the glove; that is, make sure you see the ball smack leather.

Try this. Stand with your hands resting on your knees. Have a friend stay about 40 feet away and toss you five fast-moving, low-bouncing ground balls.

Now take a low fielding stance. Field five more ground balls. Notice how much easier it is to come up than go down on a ball.

At first, you'll feel funny—almost like a waddling duck. You'll want to say, "Hey, this isn't for me." Baloney. Did you ever hear a duck complain? Certainly not. Then neither should you. Besides, you can field a ground ball; a duck can't.

Make That Throw Good

You go to the County Fair. A carnival sign reads, "Break a plate and win a prize." You pick up a ball, wind up, throw hard, and miss by 2 feet.

Did the plate move? No. Was it a trick ball? No. Then why did you miss? Too much zip—you threw the ball too hard. A quick, accurate throw breaks more plates and retires more runners than hard, wild tosses.

Here's a drill that will help you make accurate throws.

DRILL 3: INFIELD THROWS

Purpose: To practice making sidearm and three-quarter motion throws.

Equipment: Gloves and balls.

Procedure:

1. Have a friend, Player 2, stand about 70 feet away from you, Player 1.

2. Set two balls about 40 feet apart and approximately halfway between you and your friend (Illus. 31).

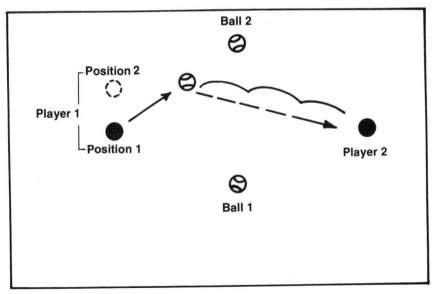

Illus. 31. Infield throwing practice.

3. Player 2 calls "Go" and tosses a ground ball to your left. Field the ball and make a three-quarter motion throw to your friend. Then break to your right, field Ball 1, and make a sidearm throw.

4. Go to position 2; Player 2 replaces Ball 1.

5. Reverse the procedure. On the call of "Go," break to your right, field the thrown ground ball, and make a three-quarter motion throw. Field Ball 2 and make a sidearm throw.

6. Return to Position 1; Player 2 replaces Ball 2.

7. Repeat four or five times.

Chasing Down a Pop Fly

It's fun to run after high fly balls. But few players smile when they fail to catch them. These fielding tips will help put a smile on your face:

● Keep your eyes on the ball.

● Move quickly under the ball.

● Set your feet. Keep your weight slightly over your toes (Illus. 32).

● Hold the fingers of your glove upward. Keep your arms and hands extended in front of your head (Illus. 33).

● Try to make the catch at about head level. Don't turn your head to the side at the last minute. If you do, you might lose track of the ball.

● Catch the ball before you try to throw it. Then get rid of the ball quickly.

Find a good fungo hitter. (A fungo hitter stands in one place, tosses a ball into the air, and hits it.) Have the batter mix hitting short pop flies with towering fly balls. Now start chasing them.

What's the best way to catch pop flies drifting over your head? You must decide, turn, and quickly run to the spot where you think the ball will land. At the last moment, look up, find, and catch the ball. (This takes some talent and loads of practice.)

Keep your ears open. Listen for charging outfielders. Be ready to duck or dive out of the way in case another player calls for the ball. Avoid collisions—they produce bumps, bruises, and runs for the other team.

Illus. 32 and 33. In chasing a fly ball, get under it quickly, set your feet, hold your glove upwards and make the catch at about head level.

Suppose They Make You a Catcher

Okay, you don't run like a greyhound and your throwing arm doesn't scare anyone. Does this mean you should forget about playing shortstop? Yes, a thousand times yes. If you want to torture yourself, stick your tongue on an electric fence, but please don't play shortstop.

Where, then, should you play? Here's a hint—try catching. What a swell deal. No bunts to worry about, no runners stealing bases, and no

Illus. 34. Catcher's stance with one knee on ground.

Illus. 35. Crouching on both legs.

mask, chest protector, or heavy mitt to wear. There's no set way to position yourself behind home plate. You can squat or crouch low on both legs (Illus. 35) or one leg (Illus. 34) or stand to one side of home plate and lean over. It's up to you.

But don't think a catcher's only job is to catch the ball and throw it back to the pitcher. Here are three big items that go with the job:

● A catcher must stay alert, encourage the pitcher to throw strikes, and help the defense by telling fielders where to play each batter.

● A catcher must be strong, tough, and willing to block home plate and stop runs from scoring.

● A catcher must study each batter's hitting style—swing, stance, grip—and try to spot a batter's weakness.

Enjoy yourself. You have the best seat in the park and one of the shortest walks to the bench.

Maybe You'd Rather Play First Base

Life's been nice to you. You've been blessed with a strong arm, fast hands, fair speed, and excellent fielding ability. Go ahead. Play first base. You should do well there.

Since a batter can't bunt in slow pitch, you'll need to play even with the bag or a few feet behind it. You'll also have to practice your footwork around the bag.

If you're new to first base, ask someone to help you. Here's a tip—don't worry about how to shift your feet around the bag. After two or three practice sessions, everything will fall into place. The following suggestion will get you started. Let's say you're right-handed—it's perfectly fine to tag the bag with your right foot and stretch out to meet ball with your left foot. If you're left-handed, do the reverse—tag the bag with your left foot and stretch out with the right foot. If you use the corners of the bag on throws to the side, you will cover more ground and do a decent job. Don't be afraid to leave the base on a wild throw. If you try to stay on the bag, a wide or high throw may allow a runner to score. Do the best you can to stop the ball.

Let's get you in shape to play first. Grab a friend, go to the nearest softball diamond and try the following drill.

DRILL 4: COVERING FIRST

1. Stand at first base (a folded towel or thin board) and send your friend to shortstop.

2. Mix tossing ground balls to third base and second base. Have your friend field them and throw easy to you. Keep working until you begin to feel comfortable.

3. Now ask your friend to speed up the throws.

4. After several tosses, tell him to mix throwing balls that bounce in front of the bag and balls that drive you off the bag to make the catch.

Practice hard. Practice often. Go left. Go right. Jump high. Really stretch out those muscles. Before long, you'll think of first base as your second home.

And don't fall apart if someone calls you "Shorty." Sure, it's nice to be a tall first baseman. But just keep hustling and the name "Shorty" will soon fade away.

Try Your Luck at Second Base

What's that? You still can't shake the name "Shorty"? Okay, how about playing second base? Before you decide, glance at the following checklist. See which items apply to you.

● Good arm.

● Fair speed.

● Crazy about fielding ground balls.

● Willing to run after fly balls.

● Super on making double plays.

● Fed up with being called "Shorty."

If these items hit home, grab your glove and come over to second base.

Now practice fielding ground balls until your glove wears out. Chase fly balls until your shoes fall off. Then buy a new glove and a pair of shoes, fetch a shortstop and first baseman, and go to work on making the double play.

Head for the diamond again. Use a towel or thin board for second base. Begin by having the first baseman flip you several ground balls. Field each ball and throw to the shortstop coming across the bag. Aim for the shortstop's glove side. Keep the ball high enough so the shortstop can handle it easily. Make sure your toss reaches second base a couple of steps ahead of the shortstop. Timing is very important. Keep working until your toss and the shortstop's come-across flow as one smooth motion.

Now switch off. Have the shortstop field and throw to you covering second base (Illus. 36). Get to the bag quickly, step on base with your right foot, pivot, and throw.

Making the double play is like eating peanuts. You can't settle for just one method. You've got to try others. For example, you can drag your left foot over the base, plant your right foot toward the mound, and throw. Or you can tag the bag with your left foot, back up, and throw to first.

Whatever method you pick, practice, practice, practice. Stay low, play deep behind the bag, and be ready to go right or left. Watch each batter carefully and anticipate where the batted ball might go.

Illus. 36. The shortstop's come-across throw to the second baseman has to be one smooth motion.

Playing Shortstop Is Okay, Too

What does it take to play shortstop? Run your finger down the following list. If you come to an item that doesn't apply to you, stop. Remove your finger. Go on to something else. You didn't want to play shortstop anyway.

● Fast hands. Able to get rid of the ball in a hurry.

● Excellent speed. Able to cover ground between third base and second base.

● Superb fielding ability. Able to stop anything from a mile-high pop-up to a steaming line drive.

● Strong, accurate throwing arm. Able to make long sidearm and overhand throws.

● Quick reflexes. Able to break right or break left without delay.

If your finger is still moving, then keep reading.

Since nearly every batter hits the ball in slow pitch, you'll get plenty of chances to field and throw. And since balls fly off the bat like rocks from a spinning tire, you must play deep—on or near the outfield grass. You can see why it takes a powerful arm to throw runners out.

When you practice making double plays and the second baseman

Illus. 37. A shortstop must be able to move in any direction and stop hard-hit grounders.

Illus. 38. He must also straighten up quickly and make strong, accurate sidearm or overhand throws.

fields the ball, do this—head for the bag, take the toss, step on the bag with your right foot, and throw. Keep the throw and stride in line with the base path toward first base. Time the play so you can throw to first before the runner reaches second base.

Again, there is more than one way to wipe out a runner. Have an experienced shortstop work with you and show you ways to improve your play.

There's Always Third Base

If you haven't found an infield position, take a deep breath. There's only one left, third base. But don't think third base is a breeze to play. No way. You've got to have a strong arm, tough body, and be ready to grab hard smashes whipping down the baseline.

A ball can't be bunted, but a batter may top the ball and send a slow roller down the line. When this happens, you must charge fast, reach down with your bare hand, and come up throwing. There isn't time to straighten up and throw. This is one of the toughest plays for a third baseman to make.

Playing close to the line can be dangerous. Watch out for the fence or other obstacles. Protect yourself by holding out your hand to slow you down (Illus. 39). This holds true for first basemen as well.

Have someone hit you hot liners near the bag and high, pop flies near the fence. Practice making throws to first and second base.

If you decide not to play the infield, move on to the next chapter. Read all about playing the outfield.

Putting It All Together

Work out in the infield. Have fun running after pop flies and smothering ground balls with your glove. Stay low as you go. And be on the lookout for blazing line drives.

Kneel behind home plate. Visit first base. Spend a day or two at second or shortstop or third. If you feel uncomfortable, move on. Somewhere, somehow you'll find a position that's right for you. And when you do, you'll have a great time.

Illus. 39. Put your hand out when chasing a foul fly ball near a fence, tree or any high obstacle.

How to Play the Outfield

Humor weaves its way into nearly every subject, including baseball. Many humorists aim their jocularity (no pun intended) at the poor outfielder. Here are a few typical lines:

Outfielders should pay their way into the game.

All outfielders graduated from Catatonic State.

Retire early. Become an outfielder.

And so on.

Do these barbs speak the truth about playing the outfield? Not in slow pitch softball. First of all, an outfielder doesn't have time to dope off. Action comes fast and heavy. There is enough running, fielding, and throwing to keep any athlete on the move. This chapter will give a clear picture of the important job an outfielder does.

What Are the Physical Requirements?

Are you thinking about becoming an outfielder? Before you decide, let's examine five fundamental requirements which make up a good outfielder.

First, fair speed is essential. An outfielder is constantly on the go, running back for long fly balls or racing forward for sinking line drives. An outfielder doesn't need the speed of a cheetah, but should arrive under most balls without having to make a head-long dive.

Second, quick reactions make the job easier. An outfielder must be able to break quickly to the left or to the right. Knocking down a ball hit to the side often means the difference between a single and an extra-base hit.

Third, an outfielder should be able to judge fly balls. This demands constant practice and the ability to be at the right place at the right time.

He must also be able to size up a batter, that is, tell from the stance and swing where the batter is most likely to hit the ball.

Fourth, a strong, accurate throwing arm is extremely valuable. For example, a fast runner can tag up and score from second base on a long fly ball. A powerful arm would discourage such a play.

Fifth, being in good physical condition is a must. The fast pace of slow pitch can wear down a player in a hurry. Hard running and long throws have a way of testing the staying power of muscles.

What Are the Mental Requirements?

Does an outfielder need to have a super intellect? No, but a player who loses concentration easily and enjoys gawking around would be better off watching the game from the stands.

What, then, makes up the mental machinery of a flychaser? A responsible outfielder should have an alert mind and know ahead of time what to do with the ball. Asking himself, "Where should I throw the ball if it comes to me?" keeps a player one step ahead.

Also, a concerned outfielder knows that running into a tree, fence, or teammate can be embarrassing—and damaging. A fielder interested in staying healthy communicates with teammates and keeps on the lookout for possible hazards.

Can You Play the Outfield?

Perhaps you're still not sure whether or not you should charge into the outfield. An interesting way to find out is to test your fielding ability. As a precaution against pulling a muscle, make sure you've warmed up properly before taking the test.

OUTFIELD TEST

1. Bring a partner, bat, ball, and glove to an open field. (Your partner should be a competent hitter.)

2. Send your partner to home plate to act as batter, scorer, and judge.

3. Go into center field. Clear the area of dangerous obstacles.

4. Have your partner hit five balls into left field, then five into right field, and five more into center field. Have him mix up long fly balls, sky-high pop-ups, and ground balls.

5. Then have him hit five blooping balls in front of you and five high drives over your head. He has now hit a total of twenty-five balls at you.

Scoring goes like this: Each time you make a clean play, your partner awards you one point. You receive no points for misplayed or bobbled balls. Trust your partner's honesty, but request an allowance for bad hops or balls hit too hard or too far away from you. Figure your percentage score by dividing the total points earned by the number of balls hit (25) and multiplying the result by 100. For example, let's say you collect 22 points. If you divide 22 by 25 and multiply by 100, you come out with a score of 88 per cent.

How does your score indicate your fielding ability? The following evaluation chart will give you some idea:

Score %	Evaluation
100 to 90	You've found a home in the outfield.
89 to 80	Stay in the outfield. You won't embarrass yourself too often.
79 to 70	Have you considered playing the infield?
69 or under	Become a catcher. Let someone else do the flychasing.

Some athletes might say that such a test is invalid since it doesn't follow the scientific method. Well, all right, no argument here except for one obvious fact—a player who has trouble catching fly balls or fielding ground balls in the outfield would be better off looking for another position (or becoming a scientist).

But if you've passed the test, we can now work on the mechanics of playing the outfield.

How to Grip the Ball Properly

A softball can be a lethal weapon in the hands of a careless outfielder. For instance, consider the following situation which occurs much too often. There's a runner on first base and the batter hits a ball into right field. The runner takes off, rounds second and storms into third base standing up. The outfielder's high; slicing throw forces the baseman to reach up for the ball directly into the path of the runner. Smack! Runner and baseman collide. The baseman, left virtually unprotected, could very easily leave the game on a stretcher.

Some outfielders jeopardize the health of an infielder by rushing their throws and failing to use a cross-seam grip which allows the ball to follow a straight path. A straight, overhand throw enables an infielder to be in a position to tag the runner. Look over these cross-seam grips and use the suggested drills to improve your technique.

TWO-FINGERED CROSS-SEAM GRIP

● Hold up a softball with your non-throwing hand.

● Place the index and middle fingers across the seams. Keep fingers spread about an inch apart.

● Let the ball rest between the index finger, middle finger, and thumb. Make sure the ball stays high in the hand (Illus. 40 and 41).

Illus. 40. Outfield throw with two-fingered cross-seam grip.

Illus. 41. Side view of two-fingered grip.

**Illus. 42.
Three-fingered
cross-seam grip
for throw from
outfield.**

**Illus. 43.
Sideview of
three-fingered
grip.**

THREE-FINGERED CROSS-SEAM GRIP

● Hold up a softball with your non-throwing hand.

● Place the first three fingers across the seams. Keep fingers spread about one half to three quarters of an inch apart.

● Let ball rest between the three fingers and thumb. Make sure the ball stays high in the hand (Illus. 42 and 43).

The fingers push forward and down as the ball leaves your hand. This action creates a backspin motion. The thumb, acting as a launching pad, supports the ball throughout the throwing movement.

An outfielder should avoid gripping the ball along the seams. This type of grip causes the ball to swerve away from the target, the direction depending upon wrist rotation and whether the outfielder is right- or left-handed. A grip along the right side (Illus. 44) of the seams will cause the ball to rotate clockwise. Conversely, a grip along the left side of the seams (Illus. 45) will cause the ball to rotate counterclockwise.

The cross-seam grip allows the ball to spin backwards in flight and follow a direct path to the target.

Practice the following drills to sharpen your ability to get the right grip and get rid of the ball quickly.

Illus. 44.
Gripping the ball this way will cause your throw to rotate clockwise and swerve.

Illus. 45.
Gripping the ball this way on the seams will cause it to swerve counter-clockwise.

DRILL 5

1. Bring a softball and glove to an open area—front lawn, street, or playing field.

2. Set the ball on the ground about 8 or 10 feet in front of you.

3. Take a fielding position. Stand with your feet shoulder-width apart,

bend at the knees, and bring your weight slightly forward. Keep your arms outstretched in front of you.

4. Run toward the ball, pick it up with both glove and bare hand, assume a cross-seam grip, and simulate a throw. As you pick up the ball, quickly check to see that your fingers rest comfortably across the seams. You only have a split second during the game to react—a long delay will give the runner time to beat the throw.

5. Repeat this activity as often as necessary.

DRILL 6

● Find a partner, go to a playing field, and stand about 100 feet apart.

● Repeat Drill 5 with this exception—instead of fielding a stationary ball, have your partner toss a low bouncing ball to you.

● Field the ball and make a chest-high return throw.

● Tell your partner to watch for sidespin. Make any necessary corrections.

● Field at least ten or twelve balls.

DRILL 7

● Repeat Drill 6. Have your partner mix tossing fly balls with ground balls to the left, to the right, and directly in front of you.

● Work hard. Keep the drill moving at a fast pace. Very few players improve with a half-hearted effort.

Making an Accurate Throw

Some players horse around during warm-ups by throwing a variety of pitches—curve balls, knuckle balls, and sinkers. They seem more concerned with their earned run average than anything else. Unfortunately, their arm muscles seldom loosen up enough to make that one good throw. Don't fall into the "bull pen trap." Use your head—and arm —wisely.

An accurate throw, as mentioned earlier, is a straight toss which puts a fielder in a position to apply a tag on an approaching runner.

Now that you've got the right grip, try these drills to help you develop an accurate arm.

DRILL 8

1. Find a partner. Stand approximately 60 feet apart and play catch. Tell your partner to give you a target by holding his glove near his shoulder area.

2. Hold the ball with a cross-seam grip.

3. Bend your throwing arm at the elbow, reach far back, and shift your weight to your rear foot.

4. Take a step forward, shift your weight to the lead foot (the one closest to your partner), and swing the rear foot around parallel to the lead foot. As your weight shifts forward, point your glove hand at the target. Never look away from the target.

5. Use an overhand throw with a complete follow-through. Release the ball with a quick wrist snap.

6. Give your partner a return target by holding your glove at shoulder level.

When your arm muscles feel loose, keep your partner and try this drill:

DRILL 9

1. Proceed as in Drill 8. Move apart 20 feet after every five throws. Continue to increase the distance until you and your partner are twenty throws or 140 feet apart.

2. Now make a single-bounce throw by tossing the ball about 25 or 30 feet in front of your partner. After the ball hits the ground, the single bounce will carry it to the receiver. Many times a long throw to home plate is necessary. The single-bounce throw will prevent overthrows and enable an infielder to cut off the ball.

3. Keep throwing until you can consistently hit your target.

Find time during the week to keep your throwing arm active. Working out once a week helps, but two or three weekly sessions does more to build strength and develop accuracy.

To Catch a Fly

That's the fun of playing the outfield—to catch a fly. And since you've decided to make the outfield your home, here's a suggestion—the next time you practice chasing fly balls, keep these points in mind:

● Face the batter with your feet spread comfortably apart. Bend at the knees and bring your weight forward. Rest your hands on your knees until the batter begins his swing.

● When the batter starts to swing, bring your arms forward and prepare to step in the direction of the batted ball.

● Keep your eyes glued on the ball.

● Position yourself under the ball and make the catch with your glove hand. Bring your bare hand around to trap the ball.

● Make a strong, overhand return throw.

Try this backyard exercise. Spend five or ten minutes playing catch with yourself. Flip the ball underhand as high as you can. Circle under the ball and catch it in front of your body. Simulate an overhand throw.

The Toughest Ball to Field

The hardest play for an outfielder to make is to catch a low, sinking line drive just off the shoe tops. A player must hesitate long enough to determine ball speed and the distance the ball will travel. If the fielder waits too long, the ball will drop in front of him and may take a bad hop. The following fundamentals will help you make this difficult play:

● Assume a fielding position.

● Line up your body in the direct path of the ball. Stay low as you go.

● Keep your glove hand out in front of your body. Turn the back of the glove toward the ground.

● Hold your arm and wrist rigid while fielding the ball. Excessive hand movement may cause you to misjudge the ball.

● Watch the ball hit the glove. Never look up to make a throw before catching the ball.

Wake up your partner. You're going to visit that empty field again.

When you arrive, go to home plate and have your partner take a ball to the pitcher's mound. Have him throw low line drives in front of you. (The backstop will save you from chasing passed balls.) If the pitcher's mound seems too close, have your partner move back several feet. Avoid diving for the ball—it's too risky. Concentrate on catching the ball before it hits the ground.

The Second Toughest Ball to Field

Hang on to your glove and tell your partner to stick around.

Now that you've caught fly balls and sinking line drives, try your skill at fielding balls hit deep into the outfield. Next to making a shoe-string catch, running back for a ball is the hardest play for an outfielder to make.

Again, go to an open field, and have your partner hit balls over your head. Use these techniques to aid you:

● Assume a fielding position.

● Check wind conditions. If the wind blows straight out, drop back two or three steps; if the wind blows to the left, take two or three steps in that direction and so on.

● Keep your eyes fixed on the ball.

● When the batter hits the ball over your head, step back, turn around, and run to the spot where you think the ball will land. This skill requires considerable practice to master.

● Turn around, locate the ball, and set yourself for the catch.

Don't run after the ball with your glove hand extended. This cuts down on speed and throws timing off. Hold the glove out only when you're sure you can make the catch.

Playing Rover in the Outfield

The tenth player, or second short fielder, on a slow pitch team answers to the name "Rover." Rover, the fourth outfielder, has the freedom to play anywhere in the outfield.

How important is the rover position? Well, suppose a team manager came up with a player shortage and decided to place an ad in the local newspaper for a rover. The ad might look like this:

ROVER needed for slow pitch team. Must be hustler, willing to back up throws in infield and have ability to throw ball to right base at right time. Call Jerry Williams after 6 pm 783-7580

The ad clearly shows that the rover position calls for an experienced outfielder who likes to run and has an accurate throwing arm. It's especially important for a rover to study opposing batters to find out which field they like to hit the ball to.

The following six situations and diagrams show where Rover plays in the outfield:

SITUATION NUMBER 1

A left-handed pull hitter comes to the plate. The rover plays closer to the right field foul line, between the center fielder and the right fielder (Illus. 46).

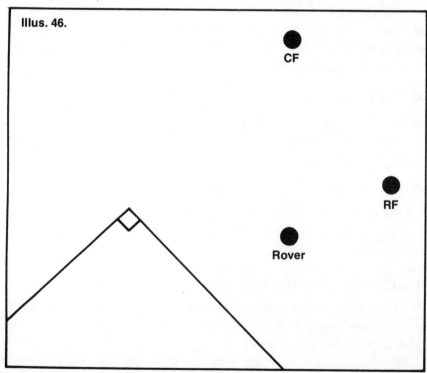

Illus. 46.

CF

RF

Rover

SITUATION NUMBER 2

A right-handed pull hitter comes to the plate. The rover plays closer to the left field foul line, between the center fielder and the left fielder (Illus. 47).

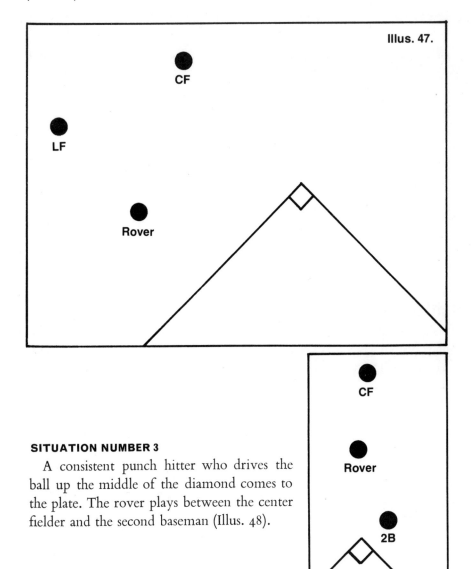

Illus. 47.

CF

LF

Rover

CF

SITUATION NUMBER 3

A consistent punch hitter who drives the ball up the middle of the diamond comes to the plate. The rover plays between the center fielder and the second baseman (Illus. 48).

Rover

2B

Illus. 48.

SITUATION NUMBER 4

A home-run hitter comes to the plate. The rover plays deep between the left fielder and the center fielder, or between the center fielder and the right fielder (Illus. 49).

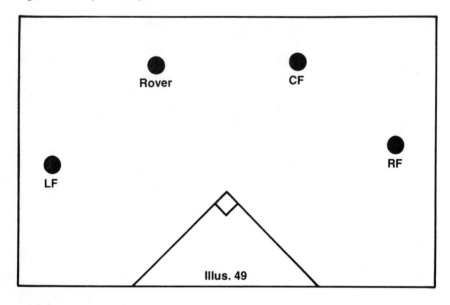

Illus. 49

SITUATION NUMBER 5

A left-handed straightaway hitter comes to the plate. The rover plays somewhere between the center fielder, right fielder, and second baseman (Illus. 50).

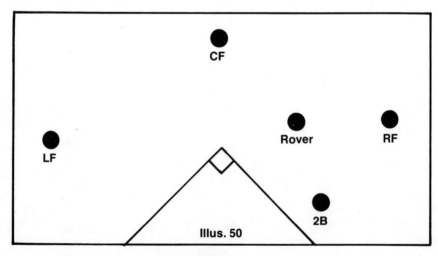

Illus. 50

SITUATION NUMBER 6

A right-handed straightaway hitter comes to the plate. The rover plays somewhere between the center fielder, left fielder, and shortstop (Illus. 51).

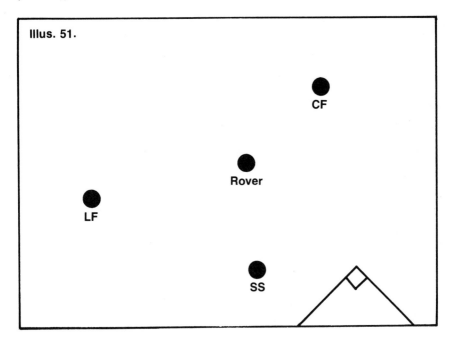

Illus. 51.

A competent manager will never use the rover spot as a dumping ground. If a manager stuck a slow-moving, weak-throwing athlete in the rover position, it would be like giving the opposing team an extra player.

Working Together in the Outfield

Outfielders, like bees gathering pollen, must work together as a unit. And like their insect friends, they must keep each other posted as conditions change. For example, an outfielder might lose a fly ball in the lights. A fellow outfielder with an angle on the ball can help the fielder by calling "In," or "Back." Outfielders should constantly remind each other where to throw the ball, how to play the hitter, and when to adjust to wind changes.

The following drills will help you and your fellow outfielders reduce confusion, save time, and make quick, accurate throws into the infield.

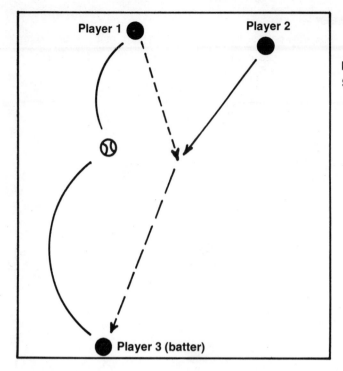

Player 1

Player 2

Illus. 52.
Setting up the relay.

Player 3 (batter)

DRILL 10: SETTING UP THE RELAY

1. Three outfielders bring gloves, a bat, and a ball to an open area in the field. Players 1 and 2 stand approximately 80 feet apart. Player 3, the batter, stays about 200 feet away (Illus. 52).

2. Player 3 starts the action by hitting a long fly ball or hard grounder to Player 1. Player 2 breaks to a point midway between Players 1 and 3. Player 1 fields the ball and makes a relay throw to Player 2. Player 2 returns the ball to the batter.

3. After two or three plays, athletes rotate clockwise—Player 1 becomes Player 2, Player 2 becomes Player 3, and so on.

4. Points to remember:

Player 1
● Assume a fielding position and be ready. Get a good jump on the ball.
● Run to the ball as fast as possible. Field it in a throwing position.
● Make a chest-high, overhand throw to the glove side of Player 2—this throw saves time and gets the ball back into the infield quickly.

Player 2
● Assume a fielding position.
● When Player 3 hits the ball, break quickly to the relay area. Hold hands outstretched about shoulder-high. Keep the glove target to the throwing side of your body.
Player 3
● Alternate hitting balls to the left, right, and straight over the fielder's head.

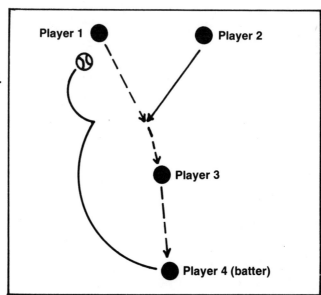

Illus. 53.
Hitting the cut-off.

Player 1
Player 2
Player 3
Player 4 (batter)

DRILL 11: HITTING THE CUT-OFF

1. Four outfielders bring gloves, a bat, and a ball to an open area in the field. Athletes stay about 80 feet apart and position themselves according to Illus. 53.

2. Player 4 (batter) hits a long fly ball or hard grounder to Player 1 (fielder). Player 2 (relay) breaks to a point midway between Players 1 and 3 (cut-off). Player 1 fields the ball and makes a relay throw to Player 2. Player 2 throws to Player 3, and Player 3 returns the ball to the batter.

3. After two or three plays, athletes rotate clockwise—Player 1 becomes Player 2, Player 2 becomes Player 3, and so on.

4. Points to remember: Review the listed points from the previous drill. When the batter hits the ball, Players 2 and 3 break to their right and line up between Players 1 and 4. Player 3, cut-off, gives Player 2 a target by holding hands high in the air. Player 2 makes a chest-high, overhand throw to the glove side of Player 3. Player 4, batter, lines up Player 3 by yelling "Go left," or "Go right."

Putting It All Together

The outfield is no place for a comedian.

An outfielder must stay awake, respond quickly, be fleet afoot, have a good throwing arm, and be an excellent judge of fly balls. A successful outfielder must spend time practicing the basic fundamentals of fielding ground balls, catching fly balls, and making strong, overhand throws to the right base.

When You Take the Mound

The desire to throw things lives within all of us. A wife, mad at her husband, might part his hair with an ash tray. A boy, stuck on a tough math problem, might throw his book on the floor. And an irate neighbor might toss the morning newspaper at a noisy cat.

Throwing things helps relieve tension and bring peace of mind. Will becoming a pitcher affect you this way? Maybe, but the only way to be sure is to take the mound.

What Are the Physical Requirements?

Look in the mirror. Pretend you're on the pitching mound ready to deliver the ball. Now wind up, step forward, and release the ball. Are you still standing? If so, you've passed the first hurdle.

Control is the second step. You must be able to throw strikes most of the time. Forget about striking out the batter. Strikeouts in slow pitch are as rare as Eskimos in the Sahara Desert. You can't throw hard enough to fool anyone. Besides, it's more fun to watch a batter swing and miss, or send a sky-high pop-up into the infield.

A pitcher must react quickly, make accurate throws to the bases, and get rid of the ball in a hurry. It also helps to be agile, able to move in cat-like fashion.

Endurance. Stamina. You need both to pitch slow and easy for seven innings. Last and perhaps least, your pitching hand should be big enough to grip the ball comfortably. A pitcher looks silly trying to shovel the ball across home plate with two hands.

Wait a minute! What about height? Wouldn't it be better to have a tall player pitch? Not really. Height isn't a major issue. If you can see over the mound and are strong enough to reach the catcher, Merry Christmas. You've found a home.

What Are the Mental Requirements?

You don't have to be a mental giant with a super intellect. You don't even need a bionic brain with psychic powers. Conversely, you'll never make a fine pitcher if you use your head for a doorstop. What does a pitcher need more than anything else? Answer: ENOUGH.

Let these five "Enoughs" help you decide whether or not you were born to pitch.

● Enough concentration to block out noises that throw off your timing.

● Enough patience or staying power to wait for the ball to reach home plate.

● Enough nerve to stand in front of hair-splitting line drives.

● Enough savvy to back up the bases.

● Enough smarts to think ahead and know what to do with the ball.

Enough said. Now throw until you fall asleep or run out of balls.

There's No Trick to the Grip

A slow pitch hurler can't get too fancy with pitches. In most cases, a batter expects—and receives—a slow, looping, underhand delivery. The batter has an advantage, but a pitcher can employ more than one grip. Study and practice the following five grips and deliveries many pitchers use.

REGULAR GRIP AND DELIVERY

Hold the ball, palm upward, with two, three, or four fingers. Illus. 54 shows a two-finger grip. Notice how the ring finger, little finger, and thumb help steady the ball. The first and second fingers rest along the seam.

A three-finger grip allows the little finger and thumb to balance the ball (Illus. 55). The fingertips are slightly spread and rest along the seam. A four-finger grip requires the little finger to touch the seam in the same

Illus. 54 (top left). Holding the ball in a two-finger grip. The other fingers help steady the ball.

Illus. 55 (top right). The three-finger grip allows the little finger and thumb to balance the ball.

Illus. 56 (right). In the four-finger grip only the thumb holds the ball in position.

manner as the other fingers. The thumb helps hold the ball in position (Illus. 56). As you release the ball, pull your fingers up and across the seam. The ball spins forward and follows a straight path.

Illus. 57 (top left). To get backspin, hold the ball palm downward with two, three or four fingers.

Illus. 58 (lower left). Grip for a knuckle ball.

Illus. 59 (upper right). With your fingertips in the seams, you can make the ball float without spinning.

BACKSPIN DELIVERY

Hold the ball, palm downward, with two, three or four fingers (Illus. 57). As you release the ball, pull up across the seams. The ball spins backward and follows a straight path.

KNUCKLE BALL GRIP AND DELIVERY

Illus. 58 shows how to throw a knuckle ball. Notice the first two fingers are bent and the fingertips pressed into the ball along the seam. The remaining fingers and thumb anchor the ball in position.

Hold the ball upward. Do not push or force the ball away from your

Illus. 60. With two fingers like this below the ball, one finger on the seam, thumb on top, you create a curve ball.

hand as you release it. Let it float or lift off your hand with little or no spin.

FINGER BALL GRIP AND DELIVERY

Hold the ball, palm upward, with three or four fingers as shown in Illus. 59. Press your fingertips firmly into the seam. Release the ball as you would a knuckle ball—the ball should float through the air, not spin.

CURVE BALL GRIP AND DELIVERY

Yes, it's possible to throw a curve. But it takes concentration, luck, and a wind blowing across the mound.

Hold the ball, palm upward, with two fingers as shown in Illus. 60.

Place your middle finger along the seam. Turn the ball so the fat, smooth surface faces into the breeze. Hold it steady. As you release the ball, create a slow, sideward spin by letting the ball roll off your index finger.

Now find a partner, stand 46 feet away, and practice pitching. Experiment. Try throwing a finger-ball curve or a knuckle-ball curve. Who knows? Maybe you'll come up with a new pitch. Above all, work hard on your control. A pitcher without control is like a driver-training teacher without a dual brake. There's no hope.

Up, Up, Higher and Higher

Official rules say a pitched ball must be delivered underhand, below the hip, reach a minimum height of 3 feet before reaching home plate, and should not reach a height of more than 10 feet at its highest point above the ground. Speed of the pitch and height are left entirely to the judgment of the umpire.

Some leagues alter the rules a bit. For example, a league in Roseville, California, allows the pitcher to toss the ball with unlimited height. Fortunately for the batter, very few pitchers choose to throw the ball more than 10 or 12 feet above the ground.

To understand why, try this little experiment. Set a cardboard box or wooden slat about the size of home plate on the ground. Stand 46 feet away. Throw ten underhand pitches at the target. Keep each pitch 15 feet or more above the ground. How many times did you hit the target? Now you see why it's tough to control a high pitch.

When you practice pitching, concentrate on keeping the ball at least 3 feet high, but not more than 10 feet above the ground.

You're Not Just a Pitcher

No siree. You must be a topnotch fielder with fast hands and quick reflexes. And you must be ready to stop line drives whistling up the middle of the diamond. Hurlers on nationally-ranked slow pitch teams know the value of keeping their eyes open and using their gloves for protection. They face guys who eat nails for breakfast and swing sledge hammers in the on-deck circle.

Gordon Wheeler, pitcher for Campbell's Carpets (Concord, California), a nationally-ranked slow pitch team, says, "You've got to protect yourself. You're standing only 46 feet away from a big, strong guy who can take your head off with a hard smash up the middle."

A smart pitcher, after releasing the ball, quickly backpedals off the mound and moves to the right or left. If the toss stays inside, the pitcher goes to that side. For example, a right-handed batter will most likely hit an inside pitch down the third base line. A pitcher would look stupid breaking toward the first base line.

We've already said that a pitcher must back up the bases. If you have a tendency to forget, do something to help you remember. Tie a string around your glove, stick a wad of gum on your shoe or chew tinfoil. Whatever it takes to help you remember, do it. Stay alert. Watch where the batter hits the ball. Then back up the base before the fielder throws the ball. For example, no outs, nobody on base. A batter raps a hit into right field. Where will the right fielder throw the ball? Second base. Where should you be? Backing up second base.

Think ahead. Talk to yourself and teammates. Always know what base to cover after the batter hits the ball. If you're confused, call time. Talk to your catcher or third baseman or shortstop or manager or bat boy. Talk to somebody.

FIELDING TIPS TO REMEMBER

These five fielding points are important and should be spelled out. So here they come again:

● Protect yourself. Let your glove act as a protective screen—keep it between your face and a line drive.

● An outstanding pitcher must also be a good fielder. A team's success hinges on a pitcher's control—and fielding skill.

● Know what to do with the ball when it comes to you. You don't have time to flip a coin or seek a fortune-teller. You've got to get rid of the ball in a hurry.

● Cover the bases. Be ready to stop an overthrow or a wild throw to the side of a player.

● Make accurate throws. It saves time and keeps runs from scoring.

How to Become a Really Good Pitcher

You want to become an outstanding pitcher. Fine, then brace yourself for some sound advice you've heard before—practice, practice, practice.

A pitcher learns to toss strikes, especially high strikes, by throwing at a target. Try this activity. Lay an old tire on the ground. Stand 46 feet away and practice throwing a softball into the hole. Have a friend return the ball. Mix tossing low and high pitches. Shoot for the front, back, and sides of the tire.

When your arm warms up, play *Win or Lose*. You get twenty pitches. Each time a ball lands in the hole, you receive two points. If a ball hits any solid part of the tire, you receive one point. A pitcher must earn a total of 25 points to win; anything less and the pitcher loses.

Win or Lose allows a player to compete against himself. Win or lose, it's loads of fun.

Making Pitching Strategy Pay Off

A thinking pitcher is a winning pitcher. You might not stop batters from hitting the ball, but you can at least slow them down. The following chart shows the strategy some pitchers use and why:

Type of Hitter	Strategy	Reason
Home run hitter	Pitch ball flat, 3 feet above ground. Throw as fast as umpire allows.	Hard for batter to swing up on low pitch. Batter more likely to hit ground ball or line drive, rather than towering home run.
Average hitter with two strikes	Pitch ball flat, 3 feet above ground.	Batter most likely to swing down and hit ground ball.
First ball hitter	Stall. Hold onto ball. Wait until last minute to pitch ball.	Batter nervous and jumpy. Determined to hit first pitch. Has tendency to swing at bad pitches.
Pull hitter with good power (Batter hits ball down base line)	Keep ball away or pitch high and inside. Move in-fielders and out-fielders accordingly.	Batter more likely to hit high, inside pitch on bat handle or pull foul.

Be very careful with a pull hitter. If you throw a right-handed batter a high, inside pitch, swing the defense to the left side of the diamond. Also, a pull hitter is more likely to hit a high, outside pitch into the opposite field.

The best time to try strategy is during practice games. Size up the situation. Move the ball around home plate. Don't let a batter see the same pitch twice. By the time league starts, you'll have a good idea of what works and what doesn't.

Variety Is the Key

Toss high. Throw low. Move the ball inside and outside. Give it a forward spin, side spin, back spin, or no spin at all. Someone once said, "Do something even if it's wrong." Good advice. The same person, watching a pitcher throw in a slow pitch game, might say, "Try something different even if you don't fool the batter."

Some pitchers look like stiff-legged robots moving just fast enough to keep from falling over. Dull. No zip. As energetic as a dead fly. A lifeless pitcher with no ambition slows down the pace of the game. No one expects a hurler to sing between pitches or dance after a batter makes an out. But a pitcher with imagination and a creative mind can challenge the batter by serving up a smorgasbord of different pitches.

High, outside. Low, inside. Ten feet high and rising. Five feet high and diving. Knuckle ball or finger ball. Keep them coming.

Putting It All Together

So you want to pitch. Good. Go pitch.

Practice your grip. Practice your delivery. Practice your control. Then practice some more.

Visit a bay or river bank during low tide. If you spot an old tire sticking out of the mud, fetch it, and bring it home with you. Now you can play *Win or Lose* but set your mind to win.

Keep awake. Don't be a "Sunday Driver" type of pitcher. Pay attention to what's going on in the game. A player more interested in the scenery would be better off selling snow cones in the concession stand.

Building a Strong Defense

Stay One Step Ahead

Arm yourself with as much information as possible about your opponent. It comes down to this—a team that knows, goes.

It would be easy to keep tabs on a player wearing a T-shirt that reads, "My name is Robert Lyle. I hit the ball a mile." But very few players advertise this way. Most prefer to let their bats and gloves speak for them.

So bring your team together as one unit. Try to out-fox the slugger, out-guess the puncher, and dazzle the young, innocent player with psychological footwork.

Sizing Up the Offense

Pitcher, catcher, infielder or outfielder—it doesn't matter what position you play. Keep your eyes open. Be a good observer. Watch how a batter holds the bat, stands at the plate, or waves to a friend sitting in the bleachers. Look for tip-offs or hints, anything that can tell you where to play on defense.

Store these bits of information in the mental notebook of your brain. For instance, let's say Player X, first baseman for Acre's Bait House, swings hard and pulls the ball down the third base line. When your team plays Acre's again, you'll have a much better idea of how to defend against Player X. If you're a pitcher, you'll probably keep the ball on the outside corner of home plate. If you're an outfielder, you'll most likely play deep, and take two or three steps toward left field. After you play a team once or twice, you get to know each player. And figuring out ways to silence a hitter's bat is half the fun. The other half is seeing how well your strategy works.

A defender may "cheat" by playing a step or two toward the line.

That's okay. You might say a batter "fudges" by poking the ball between fielders. Say it's cheating. Call it strategy. Tag it with any label you wish. But if you observe, think, and remember, you'll boost your chances of coming out on top.

How to Hold a Slugger Powerless

It's not easy. In fact, it's next to impossible to stop a power hitter from drilling the ball out of the park. Watch an open class competition slow pitch softball game. You'll quickly see why power hitters get the headlines. It's not unusual for one player to hit two, three, four, or even five homers in a game. And in most cases, the ball travels well over 300 feet.

Case in point: Campbell's Carpets of Concord, California, won the 1978 Amateur Softball Association National Slow Pitch Championship. In two tournament games on the same day, Campbell's belted 45 homers and scored 122 runs. Now that's power! At this level of competition, any player can step to the plate and jerk the ball out of the park.

Ken Sanders Ford, a team from Phenix City, Alabama, entered the same tournament with a season total of 1,308 home runs. 2,524 runs scored, and a posted team batting average of .625.

Superior strength. Brute force. Naked power. Whatever it might be, one thing shines above everything else—a slugger combines raw power with bat speed to drive the ball a long, long way. Nobody's hiding in the dugout loading the bats with dynamite or filling the balls with gunpower. The batter does it all on his own.

About the only way a pitcher can stop a power hitter is to walk the batter or hide the ball and refuse to pitch it. If a pitcher did either one for very long, he would be drawn and quartered by irate fans.

In recreational slow pitch, a team may have only one or two long-ball hitters. Let's assume you're playing on an open field, no outfield fence. What type of defense would you use against a power hitter?

Have the outfielders play 15 or 20 feet farther back than usual. It's much better to give up a single or double than a home run.

Vary the pitches. Mix tossing short and deep strikes. A short pitch barely enters the strike zone in front of home plate, a deep pitch is a high arcing delivery that enters the strike zone at the back of home plate.

But suppose you're playing on a closed field with the fence 260 feet or more away from home plate. What should you do? Again, try mixing pitches. If this doesn't work, pray for a strong wind to blow in from the outfield. When two powerhouse teams play each other and the final score reads 5 to 4, you can bet a stiff breeze clamped its teeth into the ball and kept it from leaving the park.

How to Keep a Puncher Punchless

A hurler will sooner or later serve up a batter's favorite pitch. There's no getting around it. It's in the cards. And a hitter, either puncher or slugger, will be waiting to nail the ball.

A punch hitter likes to choke the bat, lean over home plate, and poke at the ball. A puncher studies the pitch, looks for holes in the defense, and tries to hit the ball just beyond a fielder's reach. A puncher, like a forest fire out of control, is very tough to put out.

If you're a pitcher and a punch hitter comes to bat, don't throw up your glove and run off the mound. Hang in there. Get fired up. Then try these five things:

● Watch how a batter stands in the box. If he moves close to the front of the plate, pitch deep. Keep the ball high in the strike zone, near the batter's shoulders—a deep, high-arc pitch encourages pop-ups. If the batter stays back in the box, pitch short. A ball that barely reaches home plate forces a batter to lunge forward. A short, low pitch produces ground balls.

● Watch the batter's feet. Some hitters like to move up or step back before swinging at the ball. When you see this, pitch flat. Keep the ball low (but at least three feet above the ground). A flat, low pitch messes up a batter's timing since it comes in faster than a high, looping delivery.

● Change speeds. Pitch high. Pitch low. Pitch deep. Pitch flat. Keep a batter guessing. A batter who makes the wrong choice seldom hits the ball solidly.

● Study hitters. Get to know them well. For instance, if a player prefers low, outside pitches, work the high, inside corner of home plate. Conversely, wear out the inside corner on a batter who likes the ball away from the plate.

● Check a batter's hands. If a hitter uses a tight grip, pitch high and inside. Why? A tight grip restricts or binds the wrists and prevents the hitter from whipping the bat around in a smooth, level fashion. The batter has a hard time hitting the ball with the fat end of the bat.

Let's be honest. The batter will hit the ball somewhere most of the time. You know it. So does the hitter. But you might steal a few more ground balls and pop-ups out of the deal if you try different things. Perhaps a sound plan might be to think first, pitch second, and pray third.

Pick on an Innocent Hitter

Have you heard the old baseball expression, "The batter looked out"? It means the batter took a third called strike. Didn't swing. Just stood there and watched the ball zip by. Well, here's a new expression for slow pitch softball: "The batter psyched out." It means a pitcher outsmarted the hitter by rubbing a little psychology on the ball.

Granted, this doesn't occur very often. And when it does, it usually happens to a young, naive person playing slow pitch for the first time. Yes, occasionally a dab of "mind-bending" strategy stops a player cold. Let's look at four ways a pitcher might try to fool a newcomer, and, with luck, an old-timer, too.

● Glare at the catcher. Don't smirk, smile, or break out laughing. Keep a stone face. Move your head left and right two times. Then bob your head up and down once. The batter, thinking you're shaking off the catcher's signal, may lose concentration and swing and miss, pop up, or hit a ball weakly onto the ground. Not all batters realize the catcher doesn't give signals.

● Pass the word around that you throw a secret pitch. Tell everyone you only throw it when a batter has two strikes. Then just keep pitching the same way you always do. You'll find some batters swear your "secret" pitch put a jinx on them.

● Don't get into a groove and throw every pitch the same way. A hitter, big or small, feasts off pitchers who lack imagination. Let a batter see your knuckle ball, backspin, finger ball, or "secret" pitch. You might get a batter to turn psychic and start predicting pitches. A wrong guess, as stated earlier, may produce ground balls and pop-ups.

● Rub the ball, grin, and wait until the last minute to throw. A batter, thinking you're up to something, may begin to worry, call time out, and step out of the box.

Little things that bring on anxiety and raise the blood pressure of a batter add flavor to the game. And a game filled with spice is like a honey-glazed ham—mighty nice to have around.

Slowing Down the Rabbits

A fast-running team can break a game wide open by scoring a pile of runs in a hurry. A young, fleet-footed player takes pride in stretching a single into a double. Turn three or four of these speedsters loose on the bases and . . . .

Can anything be done to slow down these rabbits? Yes. With a little effort you can encourage a runner to think twice before taking an extra base. Here's what you can do:

● Be heads up. When a fast runner comes to bat, gird yourself to break left, right, forward, or backward. Be ready to take off at the crack of the bat.

● Hustle. Move out right now. Most fast runners like to punch the ball between fielders, go full speed, and try for an extra base. An alert runner knows where you're playing. Let's say you're deep and the ball comes to you. If you jog after it in a half-hearted fashion, the runner will sprint for the next base. Ninety per cent of the time a runner will beat your throw.

● Get rid of the ball. Throw it quickly back into the infield. The slightest delay signals the runner to keep going. Make hard, accurate throws to the glove side of an infielder.

Don't let a runner make you look foolish. Stay alert, go all out, and fire the ball back into the infield. A base runner recognizes—and respects—an aggressive fielder.

Talking Things Over

All right, now you know something about the team you play against. You have a bit more information than you had before. But unless you use this information to your advantage, it won't help you one iota.

In most cases, your team manager will keep you posted on certain players and tell you where to play—how deep, how far to the left or right, and so forth. You've got to keep your head in the game at all times. Remember, if a particular strategy doesn't pan out, try another. And another. And another.

There's something you should know about strategy. If it works, you're a hero. Everyone in the park thinks you're the smartest person to ever play slow pitch. But, of course, there's another side, too. Simply, if it fails . . . well . . . just tell yourself the fun comes from playing, not trying to outsmart the other team, right?

Putting It All Together

Keep your mental switchboard open. Think. Give your brain free rein to size up the other team and record vital information about each player.

Separate the puncher from the slugger. Divide the slowpokes from the rabbits. Serve up a combination salad crowded with chunks of strategy and slices of psychology.

Get together with teammates. Decide who will do what to whom and when. Then go out and do it. And, above all, have a good time.

Slow Pitch Drills
and Games for Everyone

How These Activities Will Help You Improve

The word "drill" has a way of raising goose pimples.

For example, take the young, nervous soldier going through basic training. Just mention "drill sergeant" and he'll probably snap to attention, stiffen his body, and begin to perspire. Now think about a dentist's drill. Picture in your mind the drill grinding into a sore tooth. Not too pleasant, right?

But the word "drill" holds only good things for you, the slow pitch player. And here's what you can expect from the upcoming drills and drill games:

● A way to have fun while engaging in friendly competition.

● A way to practice softball skills—throwing, fielding, and hitting—with just a few friends (five or less).

● A way to keep mentally alert and physically sharp for regular season competition.

There's nothing like helpful hints to point you in the right direction. So look over the next five items and keep them in mind as you play.

● Make sure playing conditions are safe. When necessary, wear protective clothing (long pants, etc.) and stay away from fields pitted with holes or cluttered with junk.

● In most of the drill games the pitcher acts as judge. Umpiring isn't easy. There's always somebody unhappy with a call, but try not to argue. Long, drawn-out arguments lead to hard feelings. And bickering players, like a wet blanket spread over a fire, can snuff the life out of any activity.

● The drill games allow a player or team with the most points or runs to win. Players keep their own scores. Therefore, cooperation is essential and everyone must trust one another.

● If possible, use rubber bases for drills. However, don't let bases be a problem. You can always use plywood sheets, heavy cardboard, or old rags and towels for bases and home plate.

● The pitcher must do two things to keep action going. These are: (a) concentrate on throwing strikes; (b) throw with an underhand motion and simulate game-like pitches—balls that follow a high, looping path.

All right, now you're ready. Call your friends, gather your equipment, and head for the playing field.

Practice Drills for Two Players

DRILL 12: PICK AND FLIP

Purpose: To practice getting to the ball quickly and making accurate throws.

Equipment: Two softballs and gloves.

Procedure:

1. Players stand about 60 feet away and face each other.

2. Place two softballs halfway between Player 1 and Player 2. Keep them 40 to 50 feet apart (Illus. 61).

3. Both players assume low fielding positions, arms extended out in front of their bodies.

4. Player 2 starts action by yelling "Go." Player 1 sprints to Ball 1 and picks it up. Player 2 runs to the spot vacated by Player 1.

5. Player 1 makes a chest-high throw to Player 2.

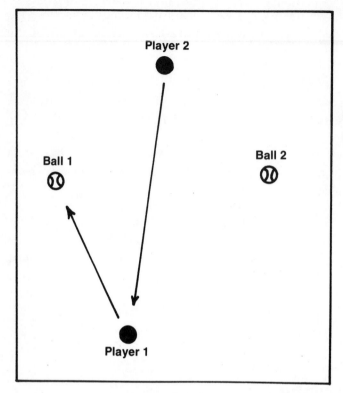

Player 2

Ball 1

Ball 2

Player 1

6. After catching the ball, Player 2 flips it to the side out of play. Be careful not to twist an ankle by stepping on a loose ball.

7. Again, both players assume a low fielding position.

8. Player 2 shouts "Go" a second time. Player 1 sprints to Ball 2 and picks it up. Player 2 runs to the spot vacated by Player 1.

9. Player 1 makes a chest-high throw to Player 2.

10. Player 1 replaces Ball 1, Player 2 replaces Ball 2.

11. After two or three rounds, players switch positions, and continue the drill. Player 1 becomes Player 2 and Player 2 becomes Player 1.

12. Both players keep fielding and throwing eight or ten times.

Comment: Keep moving. Save small talk until the drill ends. Players quickly lose interest and start to fool around when the pace slows down.

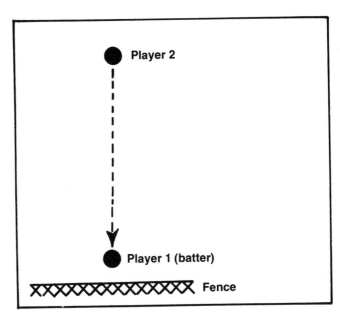

Player 2

Player 1 (batter)

Fence

DRILL 13: PITCH AND PUNCH (drill game)

Purpose: To practice bat control while carefully watching the ball.

Equipment: Softball, gloves, bat.

Procedure:

1. Player 1, the batter, stands in front of a backstop or sideline fence.

2. Player 2, the pitcher, stands about 40 feet away and faces Player 1 (Illus. 62).

3. Player 2 pitches until Player 1 swings at the ball four times. A swing-and-miss or foul tip counts as a swing.

4. The hitter should use a choke grip on the bat. A choke grip, in most cases, gives the hitter better bat control.

5. The procedure for hitting is as follows:
   Swing One—Batter punches or taps a fly ball to the pitcher.
   Swing Two—Batter punches or taps a one-hopper to the pitcher.
   Swing Three—Same as Swing One.
   Swing Four—Same as Swing Two.

6. After four swings, the batter changes places with the pitcher.

7. A round is completed when both players swing at the ball four times.

8. The game ends after five rounds.

Comment: Breathe life into the drill by keeping score. Give the batter 2 points for every successful hit. The player with the most points after five rounds wins. A successful batter watches the ball carefully and swings easy. Be a winner. Use your head as well as your bat.

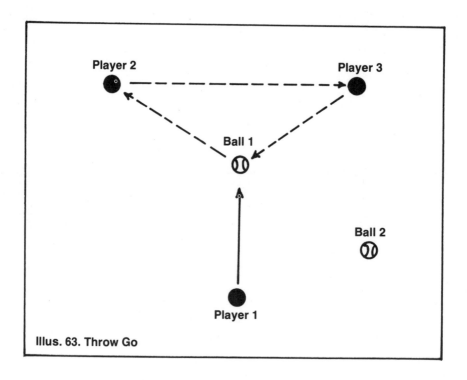

Illus. 63. Throw Go

Practice Drills for Three Players
DRILL 14: THROW GO

Purpose: To practice making accurate throws.

Equipment: Two softballs and gloves.

Procedure:

1. Players position themselves according to Illus. 63.

2. Players 1, 2, and 3 form a triangle and stay about 80 feet apart.

3. Set Ball 1 in the middle of the triangle; place Ball 2 about 40 feet to the right of Player 1.

4. Player 1 takes a low fielding position.

5. Action begins when Player 2 yells "Go." Player 1 runs to Ball 1, picks it up, and makes a chest-high throw to Player 2. Player 2 throws to Player 3, and Player 3 throws to Player 1. Player 1 replaces the ball.

6. Player 2 calls "Go" a second time. Player 1 turns, runs to Ball 2, picks it up, and makes a chest-high throw to Player 3. Player 3 throws to Player 2, and Player 2 throws to Player 1. Player 1 replaces the ball and goes back to his original starting point.

7. Each player picks up and throws both balls three times.

8. After each turn, players rotate clockwise—Player 1 becomes Player 2, Player 2 becomes Player 3, and so on.

Comment: Think hustle. Make every throw count. Bear in mind a chest-high, glove-side throw arrives quickly and can be handled easily.

DRILL 15: TARGET DROP (drill game)

Purpose: To practice fielding, throwing, and hitting.

Equipment: Softballs, gloves, bat, old towels or rags, home plate and a base.

Procedure:

1. The field is set up and the players position themselves according to Illus. 64.

2. The batter stands in front of a backstop or sideline fence.

3. The pitcher stands about 40 feet away from home plate and faces the batter.

4. The fielder stands about 40 feet behind the pitcher. He is not allowed to stand in or behind the target area.

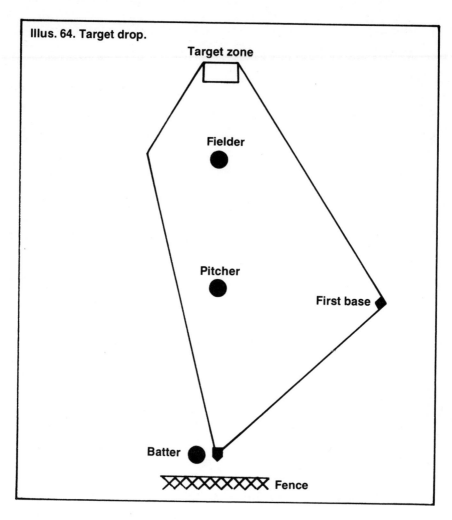

Illus. 64. Target drop.

Target zone

Fielder

Pitcher

First base

Batter

Fence

5. The target area is about 60 or 80 feet behind the pitcher. Use old towels or rags to mark off a rectangular area 10 feet long by 5 feet deep.

6. First base is even with the pitcher and about 60 feet from home plate.

7. The boundaries of fair territory run from home plate to first base to the target area to a point about 20 feet to the left of the fielder (this point should be marked) and back to home plate.

8. All players go to their positions, the pitcher starts to throw, and the batter tries to score runs.

9. If a batted ball lands in fair territory and is not caught before it bounces, the batter must try to run to first base and back to home. The pitcher covers the plate, receives the throw from the fielder, and must try to tag the batter out before he touches home.

10. If the ball is hit to the pitcher, the fielder covers home.

11. The batter cannot remain at first base; he must try to reach the plate.

12. A batter scores a run under any of these conditions:

● A fly ball or line drive lands inside or on the boundary of the target area. The batter does not have to run to first.

● The batter hits a ball into fair territory, runs to first base, and beats the throw to the plate.

● The pitcher or fielder makes a fielding or throwing error.

● The fielder at any time steps into the target area. (Pitcher acts as judge.)

13. An out occurs when the batter does any of these things:

● Misses a pitch or hits a ball anywhere outside of the boundaries.

● Attempts to bunt the ball.

● Hits a ball that is caught before it bounces.

● Hits a fair ball caught on one or more bounces and fails to beat the throw home.

14. Each batter keeps track of his own runs.

15. After 3 outs, players rotate. Pitcher comes to bat, batter goes to the field, and fielder becomes pitcher.

16. After each player makes 3 outs, the inning is over. The game is played for 5 innings or until players tire.

17. The player with the most runs wins.

Comment: Adjust the target zone to fit local conditions. If you want to make the drill tough, make a smaller target. But don't go overboard—players will lose interest trying to hit a ball into a matchbox.

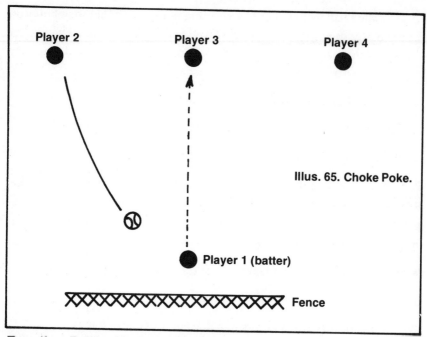

Player 2

Player 3

Player 4

Illus. 65. Choke Poke.

Player 1 (batter)

Fence

Practice Drills for Four Players

DRILL 16: CHOKE POKE (drill game)

Purpose: To practice fielding and place hitting.

Equipment: Softball, gloves, and a bat.

Procedure:

1. Player 1, the batter, stands in front of a backstop or sideline fence.

2. Players 2, 3, and 4, fielders, form a line and stay about 20 feet apart. They stand approximately 50 feet away from Player 1 (Illus. 65).

3. Fielders assume a low fielding position, arms extended out in front of their bodies.

4. Player 2 begins the action by tossing a high, looping ball with an underhand motion to the batter. The batter punches or pokes the ball to Player 3. Player 3, in turn, pitches to the batter. The batter hits to Player 4, and so on.

5. The ball moves up and down the line giving each player a chance to pitch and field.

6. The batter is allowed three hitting errors. A hitting error occurs when the batter swings and misses, fouls a pitch, hits a ball over a fielder's head, or hits a pitch to the wrong fielder.

7. If a fielder bobbles the ball, the batter starts over with no hitting errors.

8. Action continues until every player hits at least five times.

Comment: There's no secret to staying up to bat a long time. Simply choke up on the bat handle, swing easy and keep your eyes on the ball.

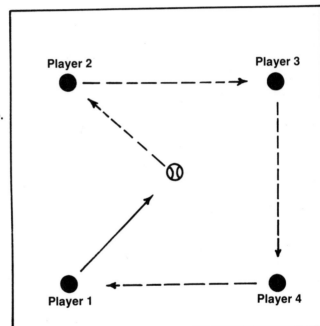

Illus. 66. Converge.

Player 2   Player 3

Player 1   Player 4

DRILL 17: CONVERGE

Purpose: To practice making chest-high, glove-side throws.

Equipment: Gloves and a softball.

Procedure:

1. Four players form a square around a softball. They stand about 60 feet apart (Illus. 66).

2. Action begins when Player 2 yells "Go." On the command "Go," Player 1 sprints to the ball, picks it up, turns, throws to Player 2, and runs back to original starting place.

3. Player 2 throws to Player 3, Player 3 throws to Player 4, and Player 4 fires to Player 1. Player 1 sprints to the middle of the square, replaces the ball, and races back to the starting point.

4. Action continues as Player 1 yells "Go." On command "Go," Player 2 sprints to the ball, picks it up, turns, throws to Player 3, and so on.

5. The ball goes around the square four times. Whenever a player makes a bad throw, play stops and the drill starts over with Player 1. A bad throw is a ball that a player has trouble handling (high in the air, low in the dirt, etc.).

Comment: Liven things up. Add a competitive factor. Try to throw around the square within a certain time. Keep the time limit within reason. Take two or three trial runs, then set the time.

Practice Drills for Five Players

DRILL 18: TWO FLAGS (drill game)

Purpose: To practice fielding, throwing, and hitting.

Equipment: Softballs, gloves, old towels or rags, home plate, bases, and two thin wooden sticks.

Procedure:

1. Players position themselves according to Illus. 67.

2. Team A, offense, consists of 2 batters, Players 1 and 2.

3. Players 4 and 5 make up Team B, defense. Player 3, pitcher, throws for both teams and doesn't come to bat.

4. Place two flag targets about 30 feet apart and approximately 70 to 80 feet behind the pitcher. You can make a flag target by tying a colored plastic or cloth rag to a 5– or 6–foot stick.

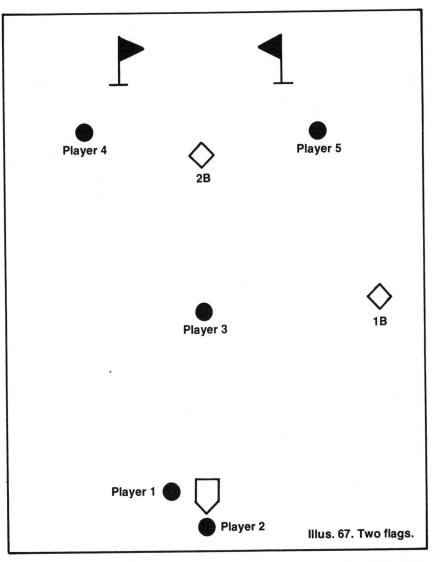

Illus. 67. Two flags.

5. Player 4 stays in left field, Player 5 remains in right field. They cannot play behind or in front of the targets. However, fielders can run toward flag targets when the pitcher releases the ball.

6. Player 3, the pitcher, stands about 40 feet away and faces the batter.

7. Use rubber bases or old towels or rags for home plate and first and second base.

8. Action begins when Team B takes the field. Player 1, Team A, comes to bat. Player 2, Team A, acts as catcher. (Batters on both teams trade off hitting and catching.)

9. The pitcher must throw with an underhand motion and simulate game-like conditions.

10. The offensive team tries to score runs by hitting a ball into fair territory, running to first, rounding the base, and tagging second before the fielder's throw reaches base.

11. Fair territory is the area which lies between the flag targets.

12. After a batter hits the ball, the pitcher runs to second and waits for the fielder's throw.

13. Both fielders stay busy. While one fields, the other backs the play.

14. Batting strategy is simple. The batter tries to hit a ball—grounder, line drive or deep fly—between the two flags. A ball which touches an imaginary boundary line (extensions beyond each flag) counts as a fair ball. Pitcher judges all close plays.

15. Team A hits until it makes 3 outs.

16. Team A scores a run when any of these things happen:
   ● A player beats a fielder's throw to second.
   ● A defensive player makes a fielding or throwing error.
   ● A fielder breaks toward the target before the pitcher releases the ball. In this case, the catcher acts as judge.

17. An out occurs when the batter does any of these things:
   ● Fails to touch first or second base.
   ● Slides into second base.
   ● Fails to beat a throw to second base.
   ● Fouls a pitch or swings and misses.
   ● Attempts to bunt the ball.
   ● Pops up or lines out.

18. Each team is responsible for keeping its own score.

19. After 3 outs, Team A takes the field and Team B comes to bat.

20. After each team makes 3 outs, the inning is over. The game goes 6 innings.

Comment: The pitcher and fielders must work well together. A co-ordinated effort based on teamwork provides a challenge to the batter. A smart hitter swings easy and tries to make solid contact with the ball.

DRILL 19: ODD OR EVEN (drill game)

Purpose: To practice place hitting.

Equipment: Softballs, home plate (cardboard or old towel), bat, and gloves.

Procedure:

1. Players position themselves according to Illus. 68.

2. Player 1, the batter, stands in front of a backstop or sideline fence.

3. Player 2, the pitcher, stays about 40 feet away and faces the batter.

4. Players 3, 4, and 5, fielders, stay about 60 to 70 feet apart.

5. Action begins when Player 1 comes to the plate.

6. The pitcher must throw with an underhand motion and simulate game pitches.

7. After releasing the ball, the pitcher calls out "Odd" or "Even." "Odd" tells the batter to hit the ball to any odd-numbered player, either Player 3 (the left fielder) or Player 5 (the right fielder). "Even" tells batter to hit ball to Player 4 (the center fielder).

8. Fielders either catch the ball or back up the play. Player 5 backs up the pitcher when Player 3 or 4 throws the ball.

9. If a ball goes to center field, the left fielder backs up the play. The right fielder circles behind the pitcher and watches for bad throws.

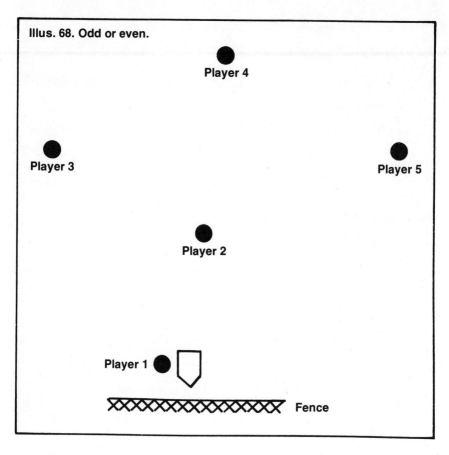

Illus. 68. Odd or even.

Player 4

Player 3

Player 5

Player 2

Player 1

Fence

10. A batter gets six swings. A swing and miss or foul tip counts as one swing.

11. A batter earns 1 point for every successful hit. However, he loses all of his points if the ball goes to the wrong field or sails over a fielder's head. The pitcher acts as judge.

12. After six swings, players rotate. Player 1 becomes Player 2, Player 2 becomes Player 3, and so on.

13. The game ends after each player bats three times.

14. Each player keeps his own score. The player with the most points wins.

Comment: Some players find it tough to hit a ball into the opposite field. Here's a tip—choke up on the bat handle, swing easy, extend your arms, and try to push the ball toward the fielder. If that doesn't work, wait until the last minute before swinging the bat.

Three More Ways to Play Slow Pitch

Lunch. Hot dogs. Suppose every day for lunch you ate nothing but hot dogs. Before long the mere thought of a hot dog smothered with mustard would make you cringe.

What do eating hot dogs and playing slow pitch have in common? The relationship is simple. If you do the same thing the same way too often, you begin to grow stale. But this doesn't need to happen in slow pitch. Variety is the key. So keep on the move and change activities often. You'll have more fun if you do.

This section offers three variations of slow pitch. They will not revolutionize the game. And it's very unlikely a new fad will evolve in the sporting world. What, then, will they do?

Game 1, *One Chance*, tests judgment and patience. Game 2, *Equal Sides,* combines the talents of both boys and girls. Game 3, *Your Choice*, allows a player to either fungo the ball or hit a live pitch (fungo means a batter tosses a ball into the air and hits it). Now let's go to the ball park.

GAME 1: ONE CHANCE

Purpose: To improve softball skills while competing for fun.

Equipment: Softballs, gloves, and bats.

Procedure:

1. Select 2 teams of 6 to 10 players each. Keep an equal number of players on both sides.

2. Team A, offense, comes to home plate.

3. Team B, defense, takes the field.

4. The game follows regular slow pitch rules with the exceptions noted below.

5. Pitcher

- Tosses a maximum of 2 pitches to each batter.

- The first pitch, Ball One, can be thrown as high as the pitcher wishes.

- The batter tells the pitcher how to throw second pitch, Ball Two. For example, a batter may call for a belt-high pitch over the heart of home plate. The pitcher must try his best to comply.

- A Ball-One strike is a pitch that touches any part of home plate. A Ball-Two strike is a pitch that crosses home plate between a batter's knees and shoulders.

6. Batter

- Strikes out under these conditions:
a. Ball One touches home plate—batter fails to swing or swings and misses.
b. Fouls off Ball One.
c. Ball Two enters the strike zone—batter fails to swing. (Catcher acts as judge.)

- If Ball One misses home plate and the batter doesn't swing, he receives another pitch, Ball Two.

- If Ball Two misses the strike zone, the batter draws a walk and goes to first base.

- After 3 outs, sides change.

Comment: Don't post a time limit. Keep going until players wish to stop. Be creative. Set up a tough defense for the hitter.

GAME 2: EQUAL SIDES

Purpose: To improve softball skills while competing for fun.

Equipment: Softballs, gloves, and bats.

Procedure:

1. Begin with a minimum of 6 players and a maximum of 10 on each team.

2. Select 2 teams. Keep an equal number of girls and boys on each team. If Team A carries 3 girls and 3 boys, Team B should do the same.

3. Team A, offense, comes to home plate.

4. Team B, defense, takes the field.

5. The game follows regular slow pitch rules with these exceptions:

● A boy player cannot use his normal hitting style. He must bat from the opposite side of home plate. For example, John B. is a right-handed batter. For this game he must bat left-handed.

● A girl player can bat from either side of home plate.

● The batting lineup must alternate boy and girl players. For instance, if a girl bats first, then a boy hits second. A girl bats third, boy fourth, and so on.

● After 3 outs, sides change.

Comment: Make any changes necessary to keep the game competitive. But go easy—too many changes only lead to confusion.

GAME 3: YOUR CHOICE

Purpose: To improve softball skills while competing for fun.

Equipment: Softballs, gloves, and bats.

Procedure:

1. Select 2 teams of 6 to 10 players each. Keep an equal number of players on both sides.

2. Team A, offense, comes to home plate.

3. Team B, defense, takes the field.

4. The game follows regular slow pitch rules with the exceptions noted below.

5. Pitcher

● Tosses a maximum of 2 pitches to each batter.

● A strike is a ball that crosses home plate between a batter's knees and shoulders.

6. The batter steps up to home plate and calls out "swing" or "fungo." "Swing" means that the batter wants to hit a live pitch, that is, a toss from the pitcher. "Fungo" means the batter prefers to pick up the ball, toss it into the air, and hit it.

7. Here are the rules for a fungo hitter:

● After the batter calls "fungo," the pitcher is free to play anywhere in the field.

● The batter must swing at the ball before it drops below eye level. This limits the batter's ability to place the hit. (Catcher acts as judge.)

● The batter receives one swing or one chance to fungo the ball.

● If the batter swings and misses or hits ball into foul territory, he strikes out.

● The batter can hit the ball anywhere in fair territory except over an outfielder's head. If the ball sails over the outfielder's head, the batter is out, and runners may not advance. This rule applies only to boys, not girls.

● A fungo batter must reach second base on the hit. If not, batter is out. This rule applies to boys, not girls. A girl need only reach first base.

8. Here are the rules for a batter hitting live pitches:

● The batter receives two chances or two swings at live pitches.

● A swing and miss or foul on the first pitch counts as a strike, not an out.

● A swing and miss or foul on the second pitch counts as a strike-out.

● If the second pitch misses the strike zone, the batter walks and goes to first base.

9. An outfielder cannot cheat and play shallow or run toward the infield when a batter fungoes. If this happens, the offensive team receives an extra run.

10. After 3 outs, sides change.

Comment: A smart hitter sizes up the defense before coming to bat. It might be wiser to hit a live pitch rather than fungo, especially when the pitcher chooses to play the outfield.

Putting It All Together

Suppose only three, four, or five players show up to work out. Do you tuck your glove under your arm and head home? No way. You thumb through this section, pick a drill or drill game, and get busy—you'll have fun while sharpening your playing skills. And that's a great way to stay physically and mentally ready.

So enjoy yourself. Play hard. And practice often.

Keeping Things Running Smoothly

Be Ready When the Bell Rings

Nice things happen when the season nears. Every time you think about playing slow pitch, a warm, springy feeling spreads over your body. It's up to you to hold the zing in the spring. And you can do it if you make an effort to:

● Prepare your body (especially arms and legs) for action by doing daily exercises. Include pulling, stretching, and lifting activities.

● Swing a bat. Hit a ball or a rolled-up piece of paper or a sponge or anything. but do plenty of swinging. Get those hands, arms, and hips rotating in unison.

● Work on your fielding. If you can't muster up a friend, take a tennis ball or soft rubber ball and toss it against the garage door. Throw high. Throw low. Stay in front of the ball. Make up games to test your fielding ability. Compete against yourself and work hard to improve your score.

When the bell rings, you won't have to look around for excuses. You'll be ready to go.

Make Way for Tournaments

Major league baseball players play their way into shape during spring training by competing against other clubs. But, as you know, slow pitch isn't the big leagues. Slow pitch teams don't go to Florida or Arizona for spring training. No, most stick close to home for their workouts.

Take an average slow pitch team. Its players may practice one or two days a week starting a month or so before the season begins and may enter a pre-season tournament to gain playing experience.

A pre-season tournament sounds wonderful. You're excited. You want to stamp your feet. Now before you get too excited, ask yourself and other players on your team these four questions:

● If the sponsor isn't willing to cough up the entry fee, will you and your teammates part with the money?

● Will there be enough players available to field a team for *every* game?

● Are you and your teammates really interested in competing this early in the season?

● Are you and your fellow players in good enough shape to go full blast this early in the season?

If everyone on the team says yes, yes, yes, yes, then, yes, enter a tournament. The ayes are in your favor.

Rules for the Team, Manager, and Player

Most recreation departments give a team manager an information sheet on slow pitch regulations for the current season. Study them. Know them by heart. Playing a game without knowing the local rules is like performing open heart surgery with a sixth-grade education. Something is bound to go wrong.

Here, for example, is what the Roseville Parks and Recreation Department, Roseville, California, has to say about game procedures, game rules, and player rules.

GAME PROCEDURES

1. *Starting Time:* Each game shall begin at scheduled time.

2. *Forfeit Time:* A team which does not field a complete team within five (5) minutes of starting time will forfeit game. A team may start with nine (9) players.

3. *Length of Game:* No new inning will begin after 55 minutes. Game time begins when plate umpire says "Play Ball."

4. *Official Time:* Scorekeeper will keep official time and will announce when there are ten minutes left in game.

5. *Home Team:* Home team is listed second on schedule.

6. *Tie Game:* If the game is tied at the end of the time limit, the game will be terminated and each team will be awarded $\frac{1}{2}$ win.

GAME RULES

Playing Rules: The current Official Slow Pitch Softball rules will govern league play.

PLAYER RULES

1. Only players on the approved roster can be used in a league game. The approved roster is on file at the Parks and Recreation Department.

2. Players may be added or subtracted during the first two weeks of each half.

3. A player may only play in one league in the Adult Softball Program. A team may only compete in one league in the Adult Softball Program.

4. Any player who falsifies information on his entry form or signs two entry forms will forfeit his right to play in the league.

5. All players in the men's league must be at least 16 years old. All players in the women's league must be at least 14 years old.

Remember the Ground Rules

Ground rules change from diamond to diamond. It's up to the team manager to know the ground rules for each park and pass this information along to the players. Each player, then, is responsible for remembering these rules.

Here are three typical examples:

● Any overthrow with ball staying in play means "all you can get."

● Batted ball hitting fair, then going into out-of-play area beyond extension of cyclone fences, parallel with first and third base lines, is a ground rule double and ball is dead.

● All balls hit into outfield in fair territory will be live.

And so on.

Let Playoffs Work for You

Sooner or later a playoff comes along. Swell. It's about time. Your hard work has finally paid off. Your team has won the first-half championship. Now check over your league's slow pitch information sheet. See what it says about playoffs. Here's how the Roseville Parks and Recreation Department handles playoffs:

1. All ties for first-half championship must be completed before the second half begins. A team will be awarded two points for each league win, one point for a tie, and no points for a loss. If at the end of a half, teams have the same total points, a playoff for first place will be held between the tied teams.

2. All players who are on the current official roster are eligible to participate in the playoffs.

3. Winner of first half in each division will move up to the next higher division. The last place team shall move down to the next lower division. In the event two teams tie for last place, the team to be moved down will be the one which lost during their first-half scheduled game.

Let's say your team wins the first-half in Roseville. Can you relax, kick back, and take it easy? Not for long. You'll face stiffer competition the second time around. Win or lose, it's always a challenge to stay on top.

How to Handle Protests

Sooner or later it will happen. You'll see. Someone will yell out, "Foul! Foul!" And, in most cases, this means protest, protest.

Okay, your team goofed. Heck, nobody's perfect, not even your team manager. So prepare for the protest procedure your league follows. As an example, the Roseville Parks and Recreation Department does something like this:

PROTESTS

Whenever a protest arises, the team manager of the protesting team shall immediately notify the plate umpire. The plate umpire then notifies the scorekeeper and the opposing team manager. A written protest containing the date, time, place of game, names of the umpires and scorekeeper, the rule and section of the Official Rules under which the protest is made and all essential facts involved in the matter protested, shall be submitted and filed by the protesting manager in the Roseville Recreation Office, at City Hall, not later than 5:00 P.M. on the following working day of the protested game, with a $5.00 fee, which is forfeited if the protest is denied. The Softball Review Committee's decision on the protest will be final.

1. If an ineligible player is playing in a game, the opposing team manager must protest the game before the game officially ends. Once the game ends, there can be no protest based on an ineligible player.

2. Protests based on a decision which involves judgment on the part of the umpire will not be received or considered by the Softball Review Committee.

3. The Review Committee is composed of one member from each of the four adult softball leagues.

Stay away from protests. They're a real nuisance, a pain you can do without.

Suspensions Really Hurt

A nasty little kid gets his hand slapped or mouth washed out with soap. Naughty slow pitch players get suspended. Don't let this happen to you. It's really senseless to act foolishly and do things that prove to be embarrassing for you and your team.

Most leagues agree that any of the following infractions may lead to player suspension:

● No person or player directly participating or involved in a game shall be allowed to have intoxicants in his possession.

● If a player who is ejected from the game by the official continues to hamper the play of the game from the spectator area, then the umpire may eject player from the park. If a player refuses to leave the park, the umpire may declare the game a forfeit and declare the other team the winner.

● No player in any of the adult softball leagues shall use profane, obscene or vulgar language in any manner at any time. Penalty is removal from the game for the first offense and removal from the league during the current season for the second offense.

RULES OF CONDUCT

Possible first-time or repeated offense of the following will result in the offending player being suspended from the league as outlined in the last item above.

● No player shall at any time lay a hand upon, push, shove, strike, or threaten an official.

● No player shall refuse to abide by an official's decision.

● No player shall discuss the decision on any matter reached by an official, except the manager or captain. During such case, the manager shall call time out and receive permission from the umpire in charge to come out and pass the foul line before the discussion takes place.

● No player shall be guilty of using unnecessarily rough tactics in the play of the game against the body or person of an opposing player.

● No player shall be guilty of physical attack as an aggressor upon any player, official, or spectator.

● No player shall be guilty of an abusive verbal attack upon any player, official or spectator.

● No player shall be guilty of discussing his personal opinion of any other player, any play or official decision publicly with the spectators in a derogatory or abusive manner.

The Manager Plays a Big Role

Gather together 100 slow pitch players. Ask a simple question: "Who wants to manage a slow pitch team?" Ten hands go into the air.

Now tell the candidates there'll be no beer commercials or talk-show interviews. Four hands drop.

Finally, get down to the nitty-gritty. Mention the things each manager must do during the season. For instance:

● Attend pre-season and post-season meetings concerning league policies and procedures.

● Look after playing equipment. Keep track of balls and bats. Sponsors frown when they continue to dish out money every week for lost equipment.

● Discuss ground rules or any rule changes with players prior to game time.

● Foster sportsmanship.

● Be responsible for team conduct. Enforce proper conduct and safety throughout the season. For instance, discourage swearing and other undesirable behavior. Do everything possible to control angry players and unruly fans.

● Help set up the field for each game.

● Call players each week and keep them posted on game time and location.

● Whatever else might come along.

Look around. How many hands are still pointing toward the sky? One? Only one? Well, that's okay. You only need one manager.

Take an Umpire to Lunch

Are umpires perfect? Do they make mistakes? A player might laugh and reply, "Does a bear live in the woods?" Sure umpires err. But so do players, managers, and fans. If umpires and players didn't goof once in a while, the game would lose some of its appeal.

Some people grumble after watching a pitcher throw a no-hitter in baseball. They claim it's boring to see a hurler mow down one batter after another. They want to see home runs and wild throws—all the things that keep them coming back to the park. A perfect umpire, like a perfect player, would, in time, drive the fans away. Remember this the next time you yell at an umpire. An umpire has a tough job. He must be a student of the game, know all the rules, maintain order, be a neutral observer, and keep the game moving along smoothly.

Be kind. If you wish to dispute a call, do so with style. For example, let's say you're called out at second base on a close play. Don't shout at the umpire. Simply rise to your feet, dust yourself off, and softly say, "Sir. I would like to express a slight difference of opinion. You see, I feel you've made a slight mistake. I believe deep within my heart that my foot touched the base before the ball arrived. Perhaps a speck of dirt flew into your eye at the last moment making it extremely difficult for you to see the entire play."

A jolly umpire might grin and say, "Yeah, I know. Nobody's perfect." But a grouchy ump might reply, "You're out! Come on, clear the base. You're holding up the game."

Oh, well, jolly or grouchy, an umpire gets hungry. So after the game, buy the ump a hot dog, a sack of peanuts, or an ice cream bar. It's not bribery. Just a good-will gesture to let him know there are no hard feelings and you respect his opinion, even though he blew the call at second.

Thank You, Mr. Sponsor

Yes, what a great idea! Go up to your sponsor, hold out your hand, and say thanks. Let your sponsor know you appreciate the opportunity to play on the team.

There's another way you can show your appreciation. For example, if you play for Jumbo Meat Market, buy a pound or two of hamburger. Or if you play for Acre's Bait House, purchase a dozen nightcrawlers. Or if you play for Benston's Used Cars, well . . . you can always sign up next year for Acre's Bait House. Let's face facts—nightcrawlers come cheaper than low-mileage convertibles. Take Mr. Benston out for a pepperoni pizza.

Putting It All Together

The season nears. You're mentally ready. But is your body set to go? Perhaps not. So stretch out those loose, lazy muscles.

What's the best way to wake them up? Practice fielding. Practice throwing. Practice batting. In short, go out and practice. But go easy and get into shape gradually. You've got a long time to play.

Stay on your best behavior. Don't be a chump and do something stupid. Who needs a suspension? The idea is to make friends, not enemies.

And, yes, the umpire is a human being, too. Try not to hassle the umpire and get him riled up. He needs a clear head to be effective.

Know the rules. Follow them. If you don't understand something, ask for help. That's one reason that you have a manager and umpire.

Last and certainly not least, give the sponsor a Texas-sized thanks. Then pat yourself on the back. You've been a big part of the slow pitch explosion.

ACKNOWLEDGMENTS

I wish to thank Clyde Bearden for his time and interest in preparing the excellent photographs and express my appreciation to Vernon, Caroline, Susan, Ken, Jeff, and Roland for standing still long enough to be photographed. I also wish to thank the Amateur Softball Association of America for permission to use some of the rules, as well as the International Joint Rules Committee on Softball.

Cover photographs by Carl Brattin, courtesy of the Amateur Softball Association of America.

Season Goal Chart

Name: Larry Brubaker

Team: Stephenson's Realty

Position: First base, outfield

Year	HR		3B		2B		Base Hits		K		BB		RBI		Runs		Sac. Flies		Batting Average	
	G	R	G	R	G	R	G	R	G	R	G	R	G	R	G	R	G	R	G	R
1978	3	2	2	2	5	3	30	26	0	1	2	3	15	18	20	17	4	2	.375	.410
1979	4	5	3	2	6	4	32	27	0	2	3	2	17	20	20	19	4	1	.405	.400
1980	5	3	3		6		35		0		3		20		22		4		.425	

G=Goal R=Result

About the Author

Robert G. Hoehn is a veteran of college, semi–pro and professional baseball and has put in 10 successful years of coaching in the Roseville Union High School District in California. A veteran writer as well, he has written four books and booklets on baseball drills and numerous articles for coaching publications including *Scholastic Coach, Coaching Clinic, Athletic Journal, Coach & Athlete* and *Sports Digest*.

Mr. Hoehn has been a devoted slow pitch softball player for the past six years in both A and B leagues and played for a championship B team in 1976. He is known around the league as "Mojo," although he confesses he hasn't the slightest idea why.